101 Reasons Why You Must Write A Book

How To Make A Six Figure Income
By Writing & Publishing
Your Own Book

Bob Burnham & Jeff McCallum

ISBN 10: 1-933817-30-5
ISBN 13: 978-1-933817-30-9

First Printing: April 2007

Published in the USA by
Profits Publishing of Sarasota, Florida
http://profitspublishing.com

Table of Contents

Attitude is everything.

– Origin Unknown

About The Authors

BOB BURNHAM

Bob started his carpet cleaning business in 1976 and quickly built it to 26 locations across Canada. By the time he was 30 years old he had 600 full and part time employees and did over 6 million dollars in annual sales. Bob sold all the locations across Canada and retained only the British Columbia locations, which were expanded into Flood and Fire restoration and are still operating successfully today. Through both the marketing of his fire and flood companies and franchising Bob has developed many marketing strategies that have propelled profits both for his own businesses and many other who have come to him for help. Bob spends tens of thousand each year on seminars, CD's and is a voracious reader to help both his companies and others achieve massive success. Many of the people he has worked with have had success on many levels due to Bob's keen sense of identifying the hidden opportunities in their businesses.

JEFF MCCALLUM

Jeff has had massive success in the Fire and Flood restoration industry over the past decade. He has been able to live the ultimate lifestyle of running a hugely successful business and much of the time only working a few hours per week in his operation. Many so called business Guru's talk about working on your business rather than in it but few have been able to truly achieve it and make it work like Jeff has. Jeff has the ultimate systems for customer services that has his customers do his advertising for him. Jeff's business has grown exponentially each year and he is recognized leader for many of his forward thinking customer service concepts. Jeff says that when your customers promote the business for you your life just gets easier each year. For the past several years Jeff has been focused on Internet marketing and has developed many marketing strategies that can propel any business to more success and all on autopilot.

Acknowledgements

This book is written with the help of many people, including some who know me well and some who have never heard of me before. It is through the many self-help, marketing, business, and non-fiction books I have read that have moulded the book you are about to read. Dan Poynter, in his book 'The Self-Publishing Manual: How To Write Print and Sell Your Own Book," states a statistic that is hard to believe in this day and age. He claims that 58% of the U.S. adult population never reads a book after high school. So it is with this statistic in mind that I want to thank you for reading this book. You are already ahead of 42% of the adult population by just reading and making it possible for me to do what I do.

It is with great thanks and appreciation that I thank Jeff McCallum, my business partner, who has given me the opportunity through his wisdom, encouragement, and support to be able to bring you this book. It would have taken years longer without his support and I will always be indebted to him.

I also have to thank my family. To Marilyn, my wife, who should be awarded the badge of honour for pointing out my strong points and believing in me. To my daughters, Shay, Lex and Sky, who are the biggest reasons for me wanting to excel so that I may be an example of unconditional love, kindness, and encouragement.

I want to thank my coworkers at ABK Restoration Services and BurnMac Services. I must also thank Sarb Hovey for all her help and great suggestions as well as Marian Turgeon of

Profits Publishing for doing such a great job on this book. All
of you are a daily inspiration to me.

Lastly, I want to thank my lawyer, Rick Watts, for always
bringing me back to reason even before I was able to do it for
myself, and to Jerry Miachika, my accountant, for his years of
work and sound advice during the good and not so good times.

Bob

They say "when you love what you do time stands still" and
it does for me everyday. With that in mind there are many
people I am grateful for: I would like to thank Bob Burnham my
long time business partner for his persistence, encouragement
and constant mentoring over the years. Without his "pit-bull"
mentality this book would not have come to life.

I also want to thank my wife Julie for her calm perspective
on everything, My sons and daughter Byron, Jeffrey, Jordan and
Amy who have been there to show me that life is truly a gift.

My Father, Dave for his years of teaching me that life is
about service, integrity and work ethic.

I want to thank my co workers at ABK Restoration Services
and BurnMac Services in particular Tim Compton for being
there when I needed him the most.

I also want to thank all the authors out there whose books,
CDS, and seminars have helped propel me forward everyday.

Jeff

What Others Say About This Book

Writing your own book is one of the quickest and most dramatic ways to attract miraculous life changes. Read this book and discover how to write, publish, promote and profit. John Assaraf, Speaker, Entrepreneur
CEO-Founder, OneCoach, Inc www.OneCoach.com www.JohnAssaraf.com Email john@onecoach.com

"After experiencing all the wonderful opportunities that have flowed my way (and continue to!) from writing my own book, I highly recommend 101 Reasons You Must Write A Book to anyone considering writing a book. You'll not only learn why you must write a book, but you'll also learn how to publish, market and make money from it. If you are an entrepreneur, coach, salesperson or consultant, pick up 101 Reasons You Must Write A book and find out for yourself all the wonderful reasons you'll want to write your own book. It's a MUST READ!"
Eva Gregory, International Coach of the Year Author of The Feel Good Guide to Prosperity.

Writing your own book has always been a great way to build your creditability AND generate leads for any business, but almost everyone gets stuck at the "how."

In this book '101 Reasons Why You Must Write a Book' you will discover how to write, publish and make money from writing your book in a simple and fast way. It's one of the big reasons why I decided to finally write my own book.

Russell Brunson www.DotComSecrets.com

"Bob Burnham has achieved something with '101 Reasons Why You Must Write A Book' that I never thought I'd see. As an author myself who writes daily, I always believed that only those people who had a talent for writing would be able to write a book themselves. I was wrong! I'm convinced that anyone who follows Bob's simple, yet effective, 'BRWT Force Technology' method of writing will be able to create a book that they would be proud of. More importantly, this method will allow you to write with ease in ANY style whether it's for articles, reports, white papers, or for blogs. I always wondered why most prolific writers never have trouble writing...it's down to what Bob will teach you about BRWT!"

Gary Vurnum, Author and Speaker
www.oursuccesspartnership.com

This book is a must read for anyone looking to further their career, life, and financial situation. It's jam packed with information not only on why you must write a book but how to write a book, publish, and actually profit from it. The action steps motivated me to finish my own book.

Annette Elton AMB Creative, LLC

I am pleasantly surprised about where this book and even though I had my hesitations, I must admit that this reading is a true inspiration. Who would have thought that there could be 101 reasons to write a book? And they are all promising. Thank you!

Jack Kyos, Lawyer, Johnson & Co. Ltd

I've been writing books for a long time now and used a lot of help from guides, but this book here is unique and probably the most helpful guide for anyone as it shows you how to make it big professionally, financially and sentimentally. Great job!

Mary Carter, University professor of English,
Hartford University

I find this reading challenging as it helps you understand how to enhance your magnetism, how to attract more business and obviously more credibility. It is also a great discussion point for my students. I will definitely recommend it to my colleagues and students.

Diana Anuja, Business University Professor,
Harding University

101 Reasons Writing A Book Will Rev Up Your Life, Career, And Your Wallet is something that every beginning or even seasoned writer should have the chance to read... This is not a straight-line "how to write a book". It is so much more as it goes into great detail and lists many reasons why writing a book can improve your life on daily basis. Writing a book, is probably the easiest way to become "famoso"!

Luis-Fernando Piron, Anchorman,
Television Nacional de Argentina

I would like to say that this book is a major influence that led me to take a position and consider writing a book. The greatest thing about what I've read is that it is user-friendly! I can really see how this book will bring me the fame and success I am looking for.

Ignacio Mantales, Marketing Consultant, Mantales&Co.

Thank you so much for writing this book! After receiving this information, I decided I wanted to make more of my career by writing a book and use all the advices found here in order to become more famous and more loved by the public. I think this book will be a blessing for everyone who wants to end being an anonymous. My music, my songs and the ideas from this book will take me a long way.

Claudia Gonzales, Singer

This book is a very well written and comprehensive manner of highlighting the benefits of writing a book. I liked how this addresses to all classes of people and how it emphasizes the idea of gaining respect, competency and attracting likeminded people around you.

Claude Methes, Professor, Pontificia Universidad
Católica del Perú

This seems to materialize into a terrific book on how to create and polish your way towards success. Now, I am eagerly looking forward to reading more and I have more confidence about submitting my own manuscript that will hopefully become a reality. "Un libro muy bueno"

Anna-Lucia Rodriguez, Manager/Owner, Capricho
Pasajero

This book is a must for those who are struggling in a very competitive market! After having read this information I am willing to declare myself the book's online ambassador. No matter what's missing in your life, you'll have the answer to your problems here!

Michael Daniels, Realtor, ProInvest LLC

Writing your own book can really help you boost your career. I was surprised to see listed here all the benefits of writing and publishing a book and I believe this guide can help everyone find a reason to write their own book. By writing a book we can share our ideas and knowledge with others.

Dr. Daniel Moore, GP, Arizona

I want you to know that you, in fact, are a best selling author!

– *Bob Burnham*

Introduction

This book has been written for two very important reasons. To help you, the reader of this book, create the life of your dreams. To further the creation of the dream life both my business partner, Jeff, coauthor of this book, and I are now manifesting.

Let me explain. I have been in the brick and mortar business of flood and fire restoration for over 3 decades. My partner Jeff joined the company almost 17 years ago. We have both done well in this business but it has not been our passion.

We have learned through seminars, mentors, coaches, books and getting the equivalent of 3 PhD's each by listening to self improvement CD's while driving our cars how to propel our company to massive success. More importantly than the learning of success principles we use in our brick and mortar business is the fact that we now know that we do in fact, through our thoughts create our own realty.

What does this mean? It means that we can have success in any way we choose to create it. Although this was available to us all along we, just like most people on earth approximately 98% of the population were just not aware of this principle. It is Bob Proctor who says the only difference between a person making $50,000.00 per year and the person who makes $500,000.00 per year is the $50,000.00 person is just not aware that he can make more.

So it is with this mindset I want you to know that you are a best selling author but you like most people are just not aware of it. Starting today you must view yourself and start being and acting like a best selling author.

I don't want you to have a goal to be a best selling author I want you to be a best selling author. The reason I don't want you to have the goal to being a best selling author is that almost all of us fail at goals. Simply put goals don't work just like diets don't work. People don't accomplish their goals because they are trying to accomplish something they are not.

If you are not thinking, being and acting like a Tiger Woods you will not be a champion like Tiger no matter how many goals your have. If you are not thinking, being and acting like Oprah Winfrey you are not likely to be a the top of the broadcasting game either. Goals will not get you there.

You must be the person you want to be now and then you will automatically start to see all the opportunities that are available to you and have always been available to you but you just weren't aware.

One of the simplest and quickest ways of being successful is to be an expert and best selling author. You will attract and see more opportunities, money and success by simply having the passion and desire to be a best selling author.

And here is the best news of all. You can do this immediately right this very second by declaring yourself the expert and best selling author because no one can declare this for you. Most people don't realize that there is no certifying board, panel or declaration from the Gods that you are the expert and best selling author.

The only person that can truthfully and honestly declare you the expert and best selling author is you. Don't wait one more minute. Declare it this second and you will be amazed and happy with all the miracles that will start to happen in your life.

How do I know this for sure? Because I have done it and I have no more qualification than probably any person that is on my customer list. I declared myself the expert and am a best selling author and I did it the day I started being one.

Remember I told you that you are also an expert and best selling author but most likely just aren't aware of it yet. Well in this book Jeff and I are going to make you aware of it and show you how and you only have to be it with passion and desire.

Why are we so passionate about this? Because this is something we can do for the rest of our lives from anywhere and everywhere in the world. This is a vocation that creates value for all and is something that you don't have to retire from. How cool is that?

We want to be a part of the journey with anyone who starts creating and being an expert and successful author and we love to hear from all of you. Keep in touch.

Follow your dreams.

– Origin Unknown

Chapter 1

101 Reasons Writing A Book Will Rev Up Your Life, Your Career, and Your Wallet.

WHY YOU ABSOLUTELY MUST WRITE A BOOK!

Fame is often a natural consequence when you become an expert at something and one of the absolute best ways to become an expert is to author a book. Your expert status will give you a higher profile, which you can leverage for years to come. Quite simply, authoring your own book is a personal and professional lotto bonanza.

Today is the day you declare yourself the expert and there is no better way to do this than to author your own book. Contrary to what most people think, there is no regulatory or certifying board that certifies you as the expert. In fact, the only person who can truly certify you as the expert is you.

Once you write a book, you achieve the expert status of an author and that can never to be taken away from you. The effort versus return for the average person writing a book can be a modern day cash generating machine and it has never been easier.

Whether you are a business person, sales professional, consultant, career employee or would be author, this is going to be the most important book you will ever read.

Now you may think this is a bold statement, or even pure marketing hype, but I can tell from experience that writing a book will make the simplest, quickest most dramatic improvement in your life both financial and socially.

How many people do you know of that have authored a book and now have their own television talk show, have experienced the thrill of their written work being turned into a movie script, travel around the country hosting sellout seminars or serving as a consultant to others? Without naming anyone in particular, I'm sure that we all can name several writers who fit into one or more of the aforementioned categories.

I have seen this phenomenon happen time and time again. I have seen a Doctor that has doubled, tripled and even quadrupled his income once he was a published author. I have seen coaches go from giving free 30- minute coaching test runs of their service, to taking only the cream of the crop clients that pay top dollars.

I had a coach who recently wrote a book about prosperity and I asked her how her life has changed since she had her book published? She told us she now gets enquiries from clients all over the world. She says she can't believe it. She has even been asked to co-host a radio program that started in January this past year and said she would not have gotten the co-hosting job except for the fact she is a published author.

Another friend of mine I was talking to told me that a few years back, when he worked for another company, he wrote a technical book about their product. He also said he could not believe the response he was receiving and he to was getting calls from all over the world. He said he was attracting fame and expert status through that book. Unfortunately, once he left the company he was not able to take the rights to the book with him because it was still his old employer's property.

Another example is of a well-known brain and quantum physics expert with a PhD that said she really started to take off and make money after she was a published author. She too was amazed at what a difference it made in her life and that:

Her Title as an Author Trumped her PhD Status

Think about that for a minute. She went to school for a total of 21 years at a cost of probably hundreds of thousands of dollars and ended up making massive amounts of money only after she wrote and published her book.

STOP THE STRUGGLE!

A book can change many lives, perhaps most of all that of the author who wrote it. When you write a book, you are producing something that has the potential to evoke emotion, thought, knowledge and possibly even skills. Whether you write non-fiction, fiction, or reference the work that you produce can affect the way your reader thinks and ultimately improve the life that you live.

Too many book authors get so focused on the closed doors from publishers that they miss the open doors of financial success that they can easily create by publishing their own book. Many authors believe that they are going to get rich from royalties, but this is rarely the case. Usually only a handful of authors make any significant money from royalties each year.

70% of books that are published each year don't even make a profit if they only rely on royalties. That, of course, is the bad news, but the good news is if you self-publish, you can easily make over six figures per year in as easy and relaxed manner.

Writing is a very respectable profession and, if it's the one that you choose, it can also be a very important stepping stone to both personal and financial wealth. Do you desire more out of life than simply working hard just to make either your boss or the company that you work for rich? Why make someone else rich when you could just as easily be working for yourself and securing your own financial future? When you work for yourself, you are in control of your own success.

On that thought, a hearty "Congratulations" is in order. You took the first step to financial freedom and unlimited wealth the minute you began reading this book. But simply telling you that fact isn't going to be enough. This book is designed to show you why, giving you over 100 reasons why writing a book is a wise idea and just how it could be one of the most important decisions you ever make in your life.

Reason 1

You Will Be The Expert

I want to start by telling you that in our society we pay a higher premium to work with and get advice from people that we perceive to be EXPERTS. This is an almost unquestionable fact for most people.

People Refer To Experts For Knowledge.

People seek out and pay premium dollars to people who they perceive to be the expert. Here is the kicker... There is no official board that certifies and appoints "experts." Many business people say that they are not experts. This is not true when you really think about it.

No matter what business you are in you, in most cases, have more knowledge about that business area than your customer. You really are the expert. Think about it, they wouldn't have called your company if they didn't think you were good at what you do.

Business people are reluctant to declare themselves the expert. They are afraid to play bigger because they think it's not yet their time. They're waiting for something to happen

- a certification, a degree, a blessing from the gods above in their industry, or a diploma to certify their expertise from their respected peers.

Expert status just doesn't happen this way and so many business people have not figured this out. The only one who really has the capacity to declare you the expert is you. Do it now and don't wait one more second.

Experts have more credibility, are more respected, more easily get media attention, can market more easily and inexpensively, are paid more, and receive less price resistance from their customers. Don't wait for someone to invite you into the expert club. Invite yourself now by walking past all the people at the back of the line.

The silver bullet and fastest way to becoming the expert is for you to 'Write a book'. Once you have written your book, you instantly have your expert status and you leapfrog yourself to the front of the line. People will look at you differently and have more respect for you. It almost sounds a little crazy, and doesn't completely make sense, but it is the way in our society that once you have written a book you are now held in a higher regard.

When you decide to become the author of a book, you also become something of a celebrity, whether you like it or not. You will then get all the additional benefits of your new celebrity status. Your world changes from chasing a dollar, to dollars chasing you if you promote your book properly.

You don't have to answer the question why, you just have to welcome all the opportunities that come along with your newfound fame. It is something to be enjoyed and to utilize for the good of all. Once you have this status you will enjoy a road less traveled.

What is an expert? Simply put, it is a word used to describe someone who is very knowledgeable about or skillful in a specific area. When you write a book on a certain topic, you are instantly considered an expert and others will trust your opinions and, in most cases, willing to pay for them.

Think about your favorite hobby. Is there a book written on it? Have you read the book and, if so, what do you think about the person who wrote it? Do you consider them to be an expert in that particular field because they wrote a book? Of course you do and, when you write a book, you too will instantly be considered an expert by your readers. You will be the one who is thought to be an authority on your book's topic.

It's one thing to have an article appear in a newspaper or magazine, but you are on an entirely different playing field when your book is available for sale in your favorite bookstore or is talked about on internet websites. When you write a book, your name and work will be forever cataloged with the Library of Congress. But, what does all of this mean? It means you are no longer just simply a writer; you are an author, and an author is considered to be an expert.

Reason 2

You Make More Money

You can easily make six figures and more each year by leveraging the fact that you are a published author. Many authors miss the financial jackpot when they write their book because they are focused on the old publishing model.

Making money from royalties can be tough, and not very many authors are able to make any substantial amount of money this way. Selling books in bookstores can be one of the worst ways to monetize your new found fame. That is the bad news.

The good news is that if marketed properly, your book can be the start of a sales funnel, which can generate huge sums of money by selling backend services and information in the same niche. Your book will be the start of a very lucrative sales funnel that could never be matched by a simple business card.

After you have written your book, it will be like a sales person working 24 hours a day promoting your good name. You are paid money for your book and it does the selling for you. Shoppers can purchase your book at anytime, day or night, online or in a bookstore and you need not do anything further. As an author, you can literally make money in your sleep.

Will book royalties alone make you rich? Probably not, but who would ever turn down money for something that they wrote years ago? The truth is that you can earn royalties years after your book is published. Wouldn't it be great to show up at work for one day and get paid for it time and time again? Publishing a book is like money in the bank for years to come.

As an author, your best source of revenue will likely derive from the fact that you will be able to market yourself as a published author and generate an impressive stream of income through information products, coaching, continuity programs consulting, public speaking and other similar avenues. What will be your most effective marketing tool? Your book, of course.

Reason 3

You Become Famous

From the day you publish, and every day after that, you will find that you will be introduced as the author of a book. You will have more people take notice of you and many will listen closer to what you have to say. You will be famous in the eyes of many who read your book.

What does it mean to be famous? The benefits can be many and can be fun. Most people will hold you in higher esteem and you will get a better response than if you hadn't published. Just as the actors and actresses that appear on your favorite television show or movie, you will be that recurring name and face for fans of your work.

When you walk into a store, do people know you? Do you wish that they did? How would you feel if someone came up to you and said, "I loved your last book?" Wouldn't that feel great? When you author a book, people will know you. They will know your name and they will want to know more about you. As a result of their interest, you may even have certain opportunities to appear on television, in newspaper and magazine articles or heard through radio interviews.

Reason 4

You Are Perceived As Smarter

The mere fact that you are reading this book shows that you are ambitious, goal-oriented and interested in improving your financial future. These, my friend, are all traits of a smart individual.

So we already know that you are intelligent and when you write a book, everyone else will know it too. As a writer, you will be perceived as smarter because everyone will consider you an authority on whatever particular subject you choose to write about. And why wouldn't they? If you are the author who wrote the book on that subject, then that automatically establishes you in your customer's eyes as the authority. The authority on any subject is always the one who is perceived as being smarter than others in the field.

There are a lot of people in this world and perception is something that, whether we like it or not, affects us all. The better perception your reader has of you will translate into a

better perceived value you give them. The way that others view
you is important, especially when it comes to your career. As
people, we can be perceived as many things and being seen as
smart is one of the best judgments that we could ever receive.

Reason 5

You Can Say Goodbye To Cold Calling

When you are a published author you are the expert, rather
than the nuisance sales person. Who would you rather deal
with? Author of the book on Easy Investing For Retirement
or Fred's Financial Consulting? I think the answer to that is
obvious to most people. You will attract clients rather than
chase clients once you position yourself properly.

Cold calling is time consuming, costly and discouraging but
once you have your client generating book your life will change.
Would you rather chase after success or have success chase you?

Cold calling is probably one of the most costly and
cumbersome ways to get sales. It is very time consuming to go
out in the sales field and knock on each door one at a time.

When you write your own book you actually automate this
system. Your book will introduce who you are with a great
first impression, as opposed to being the sales pest at your
customer's door.

Let's face it, would you rather talk to someone you have
never met before or the local celebrity who has written the book
on your business niche? I think you already know the answer
to that, and that is why writing a book can catapult you to the
front of the pack quickly in almost any business niche.

There is no question about it; a customer who is attracted to
you through your book will be a more profitable customer than
the one you acquire by your unannounced knocking at their

door. Not only are they more profitable and less price resistant, they are also cheaper to acquire.

Cold calling will only bring in customers when you are actually doing it. Your book can be bringing in qualified customers seven days a week, even while you sleep.

When you become an author, you can kiss cold calling goodbye. Why? Because, quite simply, your phone will be the one ringing. Potential customers will be the ones calling you. People will become interested in your product or service because you are the expert, the author, the individual whose work was worthy of publishing. But what does this mean? To be perfectly honest with you, it means a lot and becoming an author can open a whole new world of doors that may have otherwise been closed in your face.

Reason 6

You Save On Advertising

Once you write a book, it becomes your best advertisement. Don't get me wrong, advertising, when approached correctly, can and does work but it can also be very expensive. But your book will say one thing about you that a paid ad could never convey - it says that you have arrived adding credibility and an expert status. Anyone can purchase ad space or hand over the dough for a professional slogan, but what does any of that really mean if they don't have the product or the experience to back it up?

As an author, you are demonstrating that you have a product and information that's worthy of being published. In fact, since it is in book form, it has been already published. When people read your book, they don't need to read an advertisement about you. They already know your name and your expertise. If your book is sound in its approach and the content solves your reader's problem in some way, media outlets will look to you for interviews. Instead of you having to seek out the right publication to place a paid ad, you can save a bundle on advertising by agreeing to interviews and submitting press releases without having to spend a dime.

When you read the newspaper or listen to the radio, what do you pay most attention to, the advertisements or the news stories? If there were a large advertisement from Joe's Car Dealership promising to get you into a new ride regardless of past credit history on one page and a headline story about John's Car Dealership on the opposite page that talks about the company's history in helping credit-challenged buyers get into a new vehicle without paying excessive interest rates, which dealership would you look to first, the one who paid big bucks for the flashy ad or the one who was credible enough to have a feature story written about their service? The choice is obvious because while anyone can place an ad, it takes a certain amount of credibility to earn a feature story.

Reason 7

You Get Rid Of Your Cheap Customers

When you write a book, your time becomes more valuable and customers will realize that the type of expertise you have to offer doesn't come cheap. When you are the author and expert in your field, you offer value to your clients

There are two types of buyers that will purchase your goods or services. Some will buy on price, but others will buy on value. There is an important difference between these two types of customers. The ones that buy on price are usually the cheaper customers and are often harder to deal with. The ones that buy on value usually have more money and are looking for what your information will do for them. These customers are easier to deal with and not as price sensitive.

Less affluent people tend to buy products and services for the cheapest price whereas more affluent people buy on value or the return they will get for their money. A cheap price is not truly inexpensive if you don't get a bigger return for the money you paid. Whereas a bigger price can be chicken feed if it saves your customer some time or money or better still multiplies their money. More affluent people know this and that is why they are financially successful and these are the customers you want to attract.

Being in business for yourself is emotionally rewarding, but it also must provide financial benefits in order for it to be worth your while. Have you ever heard the old saying, "You get what you pay for?" As you succeed in becoming an expert in a particular topic, you will be able to host seminars, provide consultations and pursue other avenues that you may have once been willing to do for free. If you are trying to get your name out there, that's one way to do it. But when you become a published author, your name is already out there, so you will not be forced to continue proving yourself by giving your knowledge away for free.

Reason 8

You Attract Nicer Customers

Let's face it we are a starstruck society. When you write and publish your book, you are the star. People will want to get to know you, because they like you. Do you want to be surrounded by people who don't know who you are or people who like you?

The people who like you are just naturally going to be nicer to you.

Your book will attract people who know and respect your work. They will value your input, opinions and knowledge. As an up-and-comer, you may not always feel that your work or skills are being appreciated. In some cases, you may even feel downright cheated, both financially and emotionally, by the lack of validation or acknowledgement.

Once your book is published, both current and potential customers will instantly have a certain amount of respect and trust for you. How could you not respect someone who was ambitious and smart enough to achieve their goal and continue working to further their career? Where work is concerned, the nicest people that you will ever meet are those who truly trust and respect what you do for a living.

Reason 9

You Find Commonalities With Your Readers

It only makes sense that people who read your book are interested in many of the same things you are. No one reads books that they have absolutely no interest in. By writing your book, you will magically attract to you some of the most amazing people that want to learn and talk about the same things you are interested in.

These new found friends and you will have a common bond that will help all move forward, in a positive, in their lives. You have surely heard the saying that "Birds of a Feather Flock Together?" Your flock of birds will be inspiration to all and build upon each others successes.

When you work in any business, it's important to network with people who you share some type of common bond with. When you write a book on a specific topic, you will begin to meet people who can help you to achieve newer and bigger goals within your chosen field. This is a terrific way to get to know potential colleagues, business contacts or just share a fascinating discussion with other professionals who may be able to shine some insight on your business.

When you think about it, just by nature of the fact you have written and published your own book you are the club itself and you will attract others with the same interests. What better way is there than to have a group of people with the same interests heading in the same positive direction?

Reason 10

You Demonstrate Good Intentions

Whether you are writing a How To book that will solve some ones problem or fiction novel as entertainment to the reader you are giving great value. If you are writing your book to give great value you are already demonstrating your good intention. When you think about it there is still no better way to help more people as quickly as writing a book.

In my Toastmasters group a number of years ago a speaker gave a speech which started by asking what invention had the biggest impact on our society in the last two thousand years. There were all kinds of guesses, including computers, cars, televisions, and the airplane but no one came up with the correct answer. The answer was the printing press invented in the year 1436 by a 39-year old German man named Johann Gutenberg, and I am sure when you think about it you will agree as well.

Books took the arduous task of learning new things

and made it available to the masses. Public awareness and consciousness drastically rose with the invention of the printing press. Well, that same opportunity is available today because when you write and publish your book you can help many people all at the same time and that was made available to all of us with the printing press.

It is really amazing when you think about the fact that it was almost 600 years ago the printing press was invented and yet a very small percentage of people are taking advantage of this great invention by writing and publishing their own book. We all have the opportunity to write and publish any time we want, so decide to put your good intentions out in the world and help as many people as possible.

When you write a book, you are perceived as someone who wants to help people. What topic does your book discuss and how will it help readers? This is a question that every successful writer has to ask themselves. Perhaps you want to help people to build a house, get out of debt, choose a good college, find freebies or choose a new career path.

Writing a book that helps people will be very satisfying to you as the author and can also be a very valuable tool for your readers. When readers discover your expertise and they, along with other potential colleagues, learn of your purpose, then your intentions will be identified as good and you will become a respected expert in your field.

Reason 11

You Demonstrate Competence

I have always been amazed at the number of people who fail to take advantage of all the knowledge available to us through books. In fact, most readers do not get past page 18 in a book they have purchased. This is an amazing piece of information for two reasons. First, think of all the people that are not getting the information out of the book they bought because they fail to finish it. Second, if you write and publish your own book you are demonstrating competence by doing so.

Although I must say that the content of your book is important, it is not as important as just completing your book. Since most buyers will not finish reading it, you are still looked upon as the competent expert. A completed less than perfect book will out perform an unfinished perfect book for your competence being viewed by the general public.

Kind of neat when you think about it. You don't have to be competent to write a book to be viewed as a competent author. How many know of this little secret? In other words, get your book out there! You will be amazed.

You can have all the skill or knowledge required to write your book, but it is not necessary, because either way you will be demonstrating competency. As a writer, you are proving that your skills and knowledge are both worthy of being published and, by achieving this goal; you have proven your ability to be successful. You know what you want, you aren't afraid to go after it and, most importantly, you know how to get results. Take action and take action now!

If success is defined as the attainment of fame, wealth or social status then, as a writer, you can easily achieve all three with the right approach. The fact that you are a published author will make you famous and using that recognition to achieve greater career goals can lead to wealth and improved social status.

Reason 12

You Quickly Build A Valuable Customer List

One of the most unrecognized yet most valuable assets you can have as an author or business is your customer list. Your business' biggest cost can be in the acquisition of customers, but once they are on your list and they have already bought from you, they are like gold to you and your company.

So many business people or authors pay too little attention to their customer list and when you think about it the likelihood of your customers buying again and again compared to trying to get a new customer to buy, you quickly realize that it is much easier to sell to people who already know, love and trust you.

Many good marketers will tell you that if they lost all of their professional assets, the only thing they would need to get it all back within one year is their customer list. The fact that people are buying your book or even being given your book for free can be a great opportunity to have a system in place to start to build your customer list.

Dan Kennedy, a direct response marketing Guru, says that a customer list of 1000 people can make you 1 million dollars a year if you are a good marketer. He also says that it only takes 2000 people to make you a million dollars a year if you are a bad marketer. If numbers like this don't inspire you to put in a system to get your customer list built then you might just have an aversion to making a lot of money!

The nice thing is that when you self-publish your book you have complete say on how you can build a customer list through the sale of your books. Although you can sometimes put in these systems if you get a publisher to publish your book, you would usually have significantly less control over the process.

Another really important point here about your customer list being built is that you will regularly pull in a big one, customer that is. It is much like fishing because when you have your line in the water all the time it will only be a matter of time before you land the big one.

Your customer list should be the first part of your sales funnel and each service or product gets more detailed, bigger, and cost more for your serious customers to participate in. One $15.00 book could lead to thousands in sales from just one customer but you must be building and maintaining your list.

Once you write a book, your customers will be popping up like wild flowers in the springtime. People will want to work with you and your list of customers may go from "short and sweet" to 'standing room only.'

When you're hot, you're hot. And trust me when I tell you that, as an author, you are one hot commodity. As an expert, a speaker, a guest host, you will be the gopher in your area of proficiency. What does it mean to be a gopher? People will gopher (go for) your expertise above all others.

Reason 13

You Express What You Have To Say

When you write a book, you have full control over the contents, especially if you take the preferred route of self-publishing. You are the creator and you can express your points in any way you like. This allows you the freedom to convey your thoughts through words and/or illustrations.

As a writer, you have the ability to create words that paint a picture or spark the imagination of your readers in a way that no other tool can. Words are powerful, as is knowledge, and you can use your book to express both.

We are all unique individuals and express ourselves differently from one another. This is your chance to say something in you own words and communicate the issues as you think they should be communicated.

You never know, but your story or book can change someone's life with the turn of a single page. People are interested in your story and what you have to say and it is your obligation to put your stories and knowledge into books to share with all generations now and forever.

How many times have you had a conversation with someone only to walk away and think of something that you should have said? Let's face it. When you are an expert, people ask you questions. They want to talk to you, get your opinion and ask for feedback on certain topics. When you write a book, you can say everything that you want to say in one convenient place - your book. You will also enjoy never having to worry about forgetting to make an important point again.

Reason 14

You Become Important

What does the term 'important' mean to you? Significant, authoritative or perhaps even notable? When you write a book, you are considered all of the above. As a writer who has successfully published a book, you have earned the right to be known as each of these, and more.

As a unique person, you are already important. You are significant just because of the individual that you are. When you write a book, others will get to know you, respect your intelligence and recognize you as an authoritative figure who would write, publish, and successfully promote a book.

When you learn to effectively use your book as a marketing tool, you will notice that people are drawn to your expertise, and they value your thoughts. If you choose to host a seminar or participate in a public speaking engagement, you will walk onto the stage with an important presence. Onlookers will be thinking "this is the author." Forget about ever being an opening act again. As an author, you will be the main attraction, and all eyes and ears will be on you.

Reason 15

Others Become More Aware And Conscious Of You

I don't think I have ever seen someone who has advertised themselves on a billboard unless perhaps they are part of a bigger promotion. When you write and publish a book you are in fact advertising yourself as the expert on the subject matter of the book that you've written.

What a powerful way to advertise yourself! There are not many ways as powerful as advertising who you are and your expertise as writing and publishing your book. You will from publication date onward, be known as the author of your book and that can be used to great advantages in life not available through other avenues.

Do you ever feel unappreciated at work, or simply get the notion that your ideas and thoughts and falling on deaf ears? If so, you aren't alone. It's not uncommon to feel this way, but there is a solution. If your voice isn't coming across loudly enough, speak louder. I mean this in a figurative manner, of course, as you won't make a lot of progress by actually shouting at people. What I'm saying is that you may have to find an alternative method to get your voice heard, and one effective way of doing so is through writing and publishing a book.

To be aware of someone or something, you must first have knowledge of it. This means that you must make yourself known through your expertise, knowledge, and your ability to convey your message. When you do this, others will get to know you and what you're all about. An important part of marketing yourself and your book is through raising awareness and, when you do this, people will become more aware and conscious of your expertise.

Reason 16

You Can Help More People

In order to be successful at writing a book, hosting seminars or public speaking engagements, you must first have an angle that people are drawn to. What does this mean? Simply put, the information you are offering must offer value or be helpful to people in some way or another.

You can be in thousands of homes and minds all at the same time by the simple act of people reading your book. This gives an author great leverage to help more people at the same time and gets you away from the old business model of time for money, which can be very limiting.

Are you an expert on building houses, improving credit, getting out of debt, earning a full-time income at home, etc.? Whatever your expertise, it must be something that others can relate to and would like to achieve themselves.

Keep in mind that you can also help people through fiction writing, which are often able to evoke a spectrum of feelings in your reader. You can make your readers laugh, cry, feel suspense and/or happiness. Everyone likes to laugh, but what about someone who may be going through a difficult time in their life and reading a book helps them to relate to the topic and deal with their feelings? Have you ever been feeling blue and watched a movie or read a book that made you feel better in some way?

When you write a book, you have the ability to reach out and help people across the globe. From your next door neighbor to someone who may live thousands of miles away. Your book will have an enormous reach that is capable of stretching out and touching all types of readers from all walks of life. It's not uncommon for people to travel from other states and even countries to hear an expert speaker give a seminar or host a public speaking event, which means your potential customer base is unlimited.

Reason 17

No Competition Because Few People Are Writing Books

How many people do you personally know who have written a book? Ok, now how many of those are actually published? When you are trying to market a product of any kind, including a book, your success will be determined in some way by the amount of competition that you have.

If you write a book, you are in a class of an elite few authors who have actually 'made it' in the world of writing. You will see later in this book that anyone can write a book. If you can have a conversation with someone then you can write a book and yet there are so few people that will take the time to do it.

You will also see with our BRWT Force writing technology anyone can have a book written and published in 40 days time. This also doesn't mean that you would have to write day and night to finish it in 40 days. We will show you it is possible to do in 40 days even if you only write an hour or two per day. When you consider the upside against the down side you would have to be crazy not to write a book once you know how to do it.

It is so easy to stand out from the crowd of your competition once you have written and published your book that you will probably wonder why everyone is not doing it when they find out how easy it is. We will just keep this our little secret and tell everybody else it took years of hard work to write and publish our books.

In this instance, it doesn't really matter whether or not you self-publish or are fortunate enough to be working with a traditional publisher. Your readers are not going to know the difference. As they flip through your book, the only thing that they will care about is the fact that they are holding a book in their hands that was written and deemed suitable for publication. Few authors can claim this achievement as few are willing to take the step that you are taking today. If you are reading this book, then you are a self-starter, a leader, and a person who has the willpower to accomplish anything that you put your mind to.

Because there are few people who know how easy it is to write a book, you will have less competition as a writer. Have you ever heard someone say that they could never write a book because they don't have the patience or the ability to convey their thoughts as written words? These poor people are ill-informed and just don't have the knowledge yet that they to can join the ranks of published authors.

Why so many people look upon writing and publishing a book as out of reach for themselves, I do not know. But the one thing I do know is that you can take advantage of this phenomenon and leapfrog yourself ahead of the competition and do in painlessly, quickly and simply. It will be our secret.

Reason 18

You Will Rev Up Your Magnetism

Think of yourself as a large electromagnet switching on its raw power and attracting to you, like an enormous vacuum cleaner, people who love and adore your work. By definition, magnetism is charm, charisma, appeal, allure, pull and magic and that is really a good description of what you will experience when you write and publish your book.

If you really want to improve your presence, write a book and people will be drawn to you like a magnet. Talk about revving up your magnetism! As an author, you will be like a high-powered magnet that nobody can resist talking to or being around.

Even if you don't believe yourself to be charming, others will. If you don't always know what to say, those around you will assume that you are simply reserved. If you tend to be a little overly silly, others will just think you are quirky. Being a professional carries a certain amount of prestige that allows you to be who you are and, even if you don't believe it, charm is part of the package that others will observe when they see you.

You have probably heard that people think they know the actors they see on TV, but that is usually just not the case. You will find many people have a notion of who you are from your book, even if you are actually the opposite. You can just sit back and relax and enjoy the mystique and charisma that people think you have. Isn't that fun?

Reason 19

You Will Attract More Business

Your book is one of the strongest marketing tools that you could possibly have. Some people have business cards, flyers and even websites, but how many people have actually written a book to show their expertise? Anyone can order a stack of business cards, hire someone to design a flyer or website, but few if any are writing and publishing their own book.

I have, over the years, always gone to who I think are the experts in a field to get advice. One of the things I check for is whether they have written and book, whether I have seen them on TV, or possibly whether they have written a column in the newspaper.

When I was a young drummer, I called the drummer of the band I liked best to teach me how to improve my drumming. I now have the person who does the morning's business report on my local news, as the person who helps me invest my money.

I have probably 10 to 15 people each year solicit me, looking to become my financial advisor. Here are all these people working hard to get my business and I go with the high profile, trust and credibility person on the news each morning. I bet he has not knocked on one door or made one cold phone call and yet he can pick and choose the best clients with the most money.

You can position yourself in the same way by writing and publishing your own book. You will just naturally attract more, and better, customers. Don't tell anybody, but anyone can write and publish a book and put themselves in the same position.

If you were looking for a way to earn money at home, would you attend a seminar given by your friend who casually auctions his/her wares online or would you rather attend one hosted by "John Smith", a super seller who earns a full-time income at home and has written a book on the subject?

Aside from his impressive income, why would you choose
to attend John Smith's seminar? Is it because you consider
him to be an expert? If so, why is that? More likely than not,
you would base your opinion on the fact that John Smith is an
author. He is such an expert that his book is actually published,
so he must know what he's talking about, right?

In the above scenario, John Smith is obviously a fictitious
character. But the premise that this could happen is anything
but. When you write a book, you will draw in more business
simply because people will trust you and this, alone, is a
very strong foundation for building a business that attracts
customers.

Reason 20

You Will Gain Instant Credibility

When it comes to your career, credibility is everything. Before
they will want to do business with you, people will have to
believe what you have to say, trust that you are being honest,
and be convinced that you will follow through with your
promises.

If someone calls you up and asks for more information
on you before they do business with you, say to them "Let me
send you a copy of my book." I know a few people who do this
and it works extremely well. First it takes away any doubt that
customer had before the call and annihilates it and then puts
your credibility through the roof.

Think about the possibilities here. You do the work once
by writing your book but it keeps paying dividends by giving
you instant credibility. Where else can you get returns like
this, especially in the marketing game that can be tricky and
expensive in the acquisition of just one customer? Remember,

you can't buy credibility but you can gain it quickly and easily by writing and publishing your own book.

When you write a book, you gain instant credibility with both customers and colleagues. People will believe you, trust you and be eager to work with you. A book will distinguish you from every other professional within your field because, to put it simply, few can say that they are published authors.

Reason 21

A Book Will Boost Your Self-Esteem

Self-esteem is an inside job, but just the fact you start to write your book will build your confidence from the inside out. Your increased self-esteem will be a natural by product of you being a published author.

Let's face it, writing your own book has to make you feel good about yourself. How many people do you know that have actually written and published a book? I don't mean people that you read about or see on television, but people that you personally know. Probably not that many, but you will soon know one--yourself.

Just the fact you are referred to as an author will boost your self-esteem and it will follow you wherever you go. It is one of the best and easiest image boosters. The first time someone asks you for you autograph you will know you have reached a new level in self-esteem that you have created from the inside out.

When you write a book, it will feel wonderful to have friends, acquaintances and even perfect strangers walk up to you and mention your work. Even though you may not know them, people will know you and that feels great. In addition, you will feel smarter and you will have a sense of pride in knowing that your hard work has paid off. You knew what you wanted and you weren't afraid to go after it.

Reason 22

You Will Increase Your Communication Skills

Writing is communication in print. If you can hold a conversation you can write your book. Each time you put your conversations into print you will increase your communication skills. Writing is an important part of communication and it is a logged communication of your conversations. In addition to speaking, being able to convey your thoughts through written words, is essential to a successful endeavor into the world of publishing.

As you write your book, you are merely taking your conversations and putting them to print. Many authors get into trouble by over thinking and writing over their reader's head. The better you get at just having a good conversation, the better of a writer you will be.

Once your book is published, you will likely find yourself in a position of being able to host seminars and other public speaking engagements. In fact, you will find that people will often hunt you out to speak. Many professional and trade associations are always looking for speakers and your job is to speak and then let them know you have more information available for their members.

Don't be shy with selling your information as many people are very happy to pay you money if they like what you speak about. You can make exceptional money on selling information products after your speech.

This may surprise you, but the act of writing your book will actually help prepare you for these events. As you write your book, you're training yourself to teach the information. Speaking on the subject will become second nature to you. Writing, teaching and speaking will all work together to make you a better communicator and increase your communication skills dramatically.

If you think about it, writing is very similar to speaking. The only difference is that nobody actually hears your voice when you write. You must still pay close attention to grammar and you still need to produce words that are clear to understand. Remember conversational style will always win the race, and the hearts of your audience. When you speak in front of a group, the same holds true. The more comfortable you become in writing your words, the easier it will be to speak them effectively.

Reason 23

You Will Tap Into Your Creative Genius

You were born a creative genius but have been led astray by people who try to hold you back. Too many people have told us that writing a book is some magical power saved for only the most intelligent of our species. This could not be further from the truth. In fact too much thinking can block you from being a good writer as you will see when we go over our BRWT Force writing technology.

If you want to write a book, you will automatically tap into your creative side by just being yourself and communicating the same way you talk. Your creative genius is in the conversations you have with your closest friends. You will only stifle your creative genius when you try to overthink what you are writing about and write above people's heads.

The faster you write, the less time you have to think about it.

You don't talk slowly and analyze every word you say so why would you do that when you are writing your book. Few people would listen to you if you overanalyzed everything you said. It is the same with writing.

You will automatically tap into your creative genius by writing like you talk, and doing it as quickly as possible. I will show you later in the book just how easy it is for you to be not only creative but prolific. You will be amazed at one exercise that will prove this very point.

Not only will you be surprised at how creative you are as a writer, you will also be astonished at how fast you can write. Anyone can do it and is easier than most people think it is.

Reason 24

You Will Gain Valuable New Skills

If you have not written a book before, then you will learn many new skills as well as realize that you have skills you are not even aware of. Perhaps writing a book will be your first publishing venture. You may know a lot about a particular subject, but learning how to get it published is an experience in its own right.

The skills you will be learning are valuable skills that you can apply to many different situations. Not only are you writing your book, but automatically, by going through this process, you will learn some of the most valuable marketing skills on the planet.

Once you know these skills, you will know how to make

money on demand and all from your writing and authoring information. It is a system that has worked for over a hundred years and will work for the next hundred years. The system you will use to make money as an author is not taught in schools and in fact can be opposite to what you may learn in your writing class.

These are the skills of the minority of published authors who are making vast fortunes writing books and marketing in non-traditional ways. It is fun, exciting and can be very lucrative with more and more to learn all the time.

You will gain these valuable new skills because of the value you will be giving to your readers and the value you will be creating. It is a limitless opportunity to write your book and market and sell your information.

Reason 25

You Will Leave A Legacy

It's not something that we want to think about, but life is short and it's important to make the most of it during the precious years that we are given. A legacy is something that you would leave with someone even after you are gone.

As an author, you will create a legacy for both yourself and your family. If your children are young, they will one day learn to appreciate the hard work that you put forth to create something you can leave behind. If they are grown, they will have come to know you as a parent and as a dedicated professional. It's possible that they may even choose the same path or, at least, the same industry after having witnessed your dedication.

Reason 26

A Book Can Help You Increase Sales

Nothing happens until you have made a sale. No sales, no money no nothing. Selling makes the world go round and increases the value of things to everyone. We live in an abundant, limitless universe. Our universe is always expanding and so is your knowledge and the information you will sell.

Everyone is in sales whether they realize it or not. Don't believe me? How about the time you were trying to convince your spouse to go out for dinner or to go to a particular place on vacation. Remember trying to sell your kid on behaving better at the restaurant by offering them some sort of reward for cooperating?

We are all in sales. It is only some people's perception of sales that make them resistant to this notion. I always use the analogy of, if you are selling the right product or service to people, you are actually in the "helping people" business.

If your company has the best service, then you are helping people by letting them know how your service can help them. If you have the best restaurant, then you must help people by letting them know you have the best food for the best price. It is all about helping people plain and simple.

So, if sales is really about helping people, then why not help as many people as you can in the shortest amount of time? Makes sense doesn't it? What can be better than helping lots of people? Well I think you probably know where I am going with this one.

You can help lots of people through writing and publishing your book! And you can make even more backend sales by selling more information to people who have already read you book. The kicker is, your book will help more people and you to make more sales helping even more people. It's a beautiful thing.

Done right, your book can be a huge sales producing bonanza helping everyone that you come in contact with. Remember, it is an expanding abundant universe. Give more value than you are charging for and you will automatically become a very rich person.

Reason 27

You Create Valuable Information Products You Can Sell By Writing A Book

Your book can be the starting point to make further more profitable information products that you can take directly from your book. Making money from the sale of your book is great but it is really only the beginning in a very lucrative sales funnel you can implement once you are a published author and expert in your field.

From your book you can put together additional products such as coaching programs, home study courses, seminars, teleseminars and continuity program etc. These information products are extremely profitable and can all come from your book after you position yourself as the expert.

If you have good information and content in your book customers will always want more information from you on how they can better use and implement the information they have already gotten from you. It is a never ending process of growing information for both you and your customer that will help them solve their problem, make more money or live a better stress free life etc.

You can even get your information from your customers by

asking them what their most pressing problems are and then find ways to solve them. This is valuable information to people who have pressing questions or problems. Customers will pay good money to you for this information in all different formats.

You can sell your book as a paperback or put it into an audiobook and sell it as a 6 CD set for more money. You can also take that 6 CD set and include a workbook and sell if as a home study course for even more money. Another way is to take your book information and make it a one or two day seminar for an even bigger profit.

The best part about this is the fact that once you make your information product, you can sell it over and over and over again. This removes you totally from the time for money business model that so many people are stuck in. You do it once and get paid unlimited times. That's how to make real money.

You can probably see by now that the possibilities are virtually endless and only limited by your imagination. You can even acquire more valuable information from your customers by having a contest for the best marketing method they use. This is now information available to all your customers and you did not even have to come up with the idea. How cool is that?

Reason 28

You Will Have The Most Powerful Business Card

Almost everyone has a business card but very few of your competitors are an author. Making your business card stand out from the competition is very difficult, but standing out from the competition because you are an author is a slam dunk.

I have been in business for well over three decades and I

have never had someone hand me their book as a business card. The opportunity to stand out is simple and almost no one is utilizing this very unique market leverage tool.

The people that are using books as a business card and marketing tool are so far ahead of the crowd that they quickly have much bigger and better business opportunities available because of this method. Think of the leverage you have when you present your client or customer your book.

Who are they going to remember and who are they going to do business with? In almost all cases it will be you because you are the expert and author.

Reason 29

You Will Have The Power To Change Your Future

As the author of your own book, you are in the driver's seat to creating the life of your dreams. On some level, you have always been in the driver's seat, but you will find it even more evident after authoring your own book. More opportunities will naturally come to you and you will have more choices and better choices.

The power you gain through the new opportunities you gain, will transform your future to new heights. By the authoring of your book you change your futures course for the better and magically attract the power to determine your own successful lifestyle on your terms.

You are planting a very powerful seed of opportunity that will keep working on your behalf. Just like planting an oak tree, nature and the universe will carefully nurture your best future for decades to come, and a lot of it will come to you on autopilot.

From the very first thought of your book you are drawing upon universal laws that will manifest a better life for you and they will continue to expand as time goes by. Take the first powerful step to a better future and start to write your book today.

Who knew that a single writing pen or a computer keyboard would have so much power? When you choose to market yourself as an expert by writing, these are the many privileges that will soon be available to you.

Reason 30

You Will Experience Increased Random Opportunities

When your book is in the hands of many, you will be exposed to more opportunities. Each book you sell compounds your chances of more random opportunities coming to you. Your book will still be a creating entity long after you have finished writing it.

Your book can be your public relations firm that keeps working for you 24 hours a day 7 days a week, and never calls in sick. I know of authors that have received calls from all over the world with different opportunities, all because they have written a book.

The opportunities I am talking about would quite often not be available to people who have not written a book. In fact, a coach I know said point blank that she would not have gotten the job as a radio co-host if it was not for the fact she was the author of a book.

When you have all your book salesmen out in the universe working for you, your random opportunities will take a huge leap in numbers. Doors that you never thought would open to you are now open in previously hard to imagine opportunities.

Not only will there be more random opportunities, but you will find the quality and nature of the opportunities to be more significant than you may have been offered in the past. Write and publish your book and get your army of public relations and sales people attracting the magic to you that you deserve and have created.

Reason 31

A Book Creates A Professional Image

By definition, a professional is someone who has a particular competence in a specific area. As an author, you will create a professional image without even having to open your mouth. In many ways, your book will speak for you, your intelligence and your abilities as an expert.

We all watch the news from time to time. Have you ever noticed that many of the televised news segments feature guest speakers? How many of those speakers are authors? Most likely, there are quiet a few.

When the newscast looks for experts on any topic they usually look for the author of a book on that topic. They do that for the very important reason that it shows the person they are going to interview will project a professional image and a similar impression is automatically attached to you because you are the author of the book.

In many cases, the journalists themselves are published authors. It makes you wonder why so many people who are in the public eye want to write their own book. One possible reason is because, in addition to earning extra money, it increases their persona as a professional, an expert, an authority. Yes, an author is perceived as all of these things and the job title creates a favorable and accomplished image for those who are up to the task.

Reason 32

A Book Gives You Recognition

When you write a book, people get to know you. They will come to know and recognize your name, work and signature writing style. Not only that, but you will also be known as an expert in your field. Recognition is a form of acknowledgment and getting your name out there as a successful writer will make others aware of you.

When you think about the recognition aspect of writing a book, it is quite incredible. You gain recognition in many fields and with many people and have never met any of them. How else can you get recognized without going out into the world except through the authoring of a book?

How would you feel if your name was constantly popping up in local newspapers, trade magazines and even on broadcast radio/television? As an author, the media will want to write about you and there really is no better form of recognition than that which is earned. Some people have notoriety simply because of who they are or where they are from but as an author, you will earn your recognition through hard work and determination by being an expert who shares their knowledge with the world.

Reason 33

A Book Separates You From The Competition

How many times have you opened up your local paper and seen an ad for XYZ Insurance agency of XYZ Mortgage Brokers telling of their company's products and services? I bet you see those types of ads all the time. They can not only be expensive but are quite often not very effective.

Now how often do you see that the author of the book "How To Save Thousands Each Year From Little Known Insurance Secrets," is giving away a free special report, which you can get by calling his office. I bet you hardly ever see ads like that and yet they can be extremely effective in attracting some of the best customers.

You have totally separated yourself from the competition easily and effectively. You are so far ahead of the competition in this regard they can't figure out what's going on. The likelihood of them authoring a book is almost nil because they don't know what you know.

They don't know how easy it is to write a book with our system and even if they wrote a book they don't know the best way to position the book to get the best response. You will be the only competitor for a good long time, and be way out in front of your competition.

You probably have a better chance of winning the lottery than your competition being able to figure out how you attract all the best clients. Your competition has no idea how a book can radically change their business and we are going to keep it our little secret.

Reason 34

Opens The Entire World To Your Market

You will have the whole wide world at your door step. Most books are distributed worldwide, including both online and traditional bookstores. If you self-publish using a POD (Print On Demand) publisher, your title will be assigned an ISBN and will be available for order at major bookstores everywhere. What does this mean? Literally, a world of customers will be able to purchase your book.

If you are an expert in earning money at home, for instance, perhaps you will find even more success with your information products, seminars and other speaking engagements locally. But, think about how much different your world would be if you could reach millions of customers instead of just a few hundred.

When your book goes global, you could be paving the way for your ability to host seminars all across America or even worldwide with guests traveling mile after mile just to hear what you have to say. If it weren't for your book being available to them, how would a world of customers otherwise come to know about you?

It's great to have a local following, but it's even better to expand your career to include more readers and an increased cash flow. In the case of business, the farther your reach, the better your profit potential.

Reason 35

A Book Can Lead To

A Speaking Career

A speaking career can be one of the highest paid professions in the world. Just ask John Childers from Florida who teaches you how to make money from the platform. He regularly makes over six figures a speech by selling his information from the platform and does not charge the regular keynote speaking fee.

John makes most of his money speaking for free and selling his information products by speaking from the platform. He regularly has a herd of buyers following him to the back of the room to by his products after his speech.

I have taken his Million Dollar Speaker training and highly recommend it. Check it out for yourself at: http://www.johnchilders.com/speakertraining.htm

The nice thing about the fact that you are an author is that you will be almost 75% of the way to making some incredible dollars in a speaking career.

When John Childers tells you that this is the highest paid profession in the world you'll want to listen. He walks his talk and he shows you how selling your information, products from the speaking platform, is a whole new revenue source you just won't want to miss.

Once again, this is an area that your competition has no idea about and the opportunities to make some extreme money are wide open. Make sure you tell John I sent you if you end up taking his course. It will be one of the best things you have done in your life.

Reason 36

Expanding Referral Source

Okay, you sell your book to one customer but the sales don't stop there. If that a customer likes the content and information in your book they will refer you and many will just pass on your book to their friends or business associates.

You can have several good referrals and sales from the sale of just one book in the right circle of influence. Have you seen anyone pass around a print advertisement? You might every once in a while, but passing around a good book is a lot more common and much more profitable for you.

Don't forget, the more of your books out there, the more chance you have for some really big referrals. It is a numbers game that is dramatically increased in your favor when you are the author of a book.

Your book is a ready and willing salesman telling your story about who you are and it will not get tired, sick or just plain lazy. Your book will have the exact same message each time someone is referred to your book and the chances of them being a new customer for you are very high.

Books also don't get thrown away like magazines or newspapers and can stay and circulate around people's homes and libraries for decades. The shelf life of your book can be longer than the best salesperson you could ever hire. Anytime you can have a marketing tool work for you entirely on auto-pilot, you want to leverage that tool to the max.

Reason 37

You Will Have The Ability To Inspire Others

Just by virtue of writing your book, you are inspiring many others. I say this with a humble heart and gratitude, but the fact is that if I can write a book then you can too. I am sure anyone who has known me personally would agree that if I can do it, you can too and this is how you can inspire your core group of friends right away.

Announce that you are writing a book to your friends and business associates. You will have a few that are a bit supportive and maybe more that will giggle behind your back. But here's the deal. When you actually have your book written and published, you will be an inspiration to all of those same people.

When you are successful as a result of your book you will be helping more people live their dream just by the example that you set. Success breeds success, so it is our duty to inspire and this is one of the best and don't tell anyone but also the easiest once you learn our system.

One of the benefits of inspiring others is that they will never ever forget who you are because you have in some way touched them and improved their lives. Be the change that you want to see.

Reason 38

You Can Enjoy Increased
Travel Opportunities

Bonus! I don't know about you, but I love to travel and see the world and if I can do that and still get paid for it, it is a beautiful thing. Would you love to see the world, but are restricted to an 8-hour work day or your boss's convenience? As an author, you will have the opportunity to travel whenever and wherever you want.

Often, if you play your cards right you will also be given first class accommodation. I mean, think about it. No one is going to put the invited author in bottom tier accommodations. All expense paid and first class can be the rule of the day. I don't know of a better way to see the world.

By systematically promoting your book in the right venue in different countries you will be a frequent guest of Five Star hotels worldwide. Ten properly done press releases can net you a family vacation in an exotic local, all courtesy of your new found fame as an author.

This can all be made possible when you think outside the marketing box and nix the conventional book publishing route for the more profitable self-publishing route. You call the shots, you make the money and you determine your future. If your future has travel in it, then this is the way to do it and have your clients, customers and fans pay the expenses.

Reason 39

Better Tax Advantages

I have been in business for a long time and I have yet to see a better deal tax wise than what the government will give you if you are in business for yourself. Naturally if you write and publish your own book you qualify as being in business for yourself with all the tax benefits that go along with that privilege.

One of the most significant is that of the deductions that you are permitted to claim as a result of a running your business from your home. As an author, you may be able to deduct expenses related to the cost of a computer, internet service, office equipment (fax machine, computer printer and scanner) and furniture, computer hardware and software as it relates directly to your job, etc.

In addition, you may be able to deduct certain expenses for the business use of your home. Among them, depreciation for business equipment that you use in daily work operations. In some cases, you may also be able to deduct utilities that are used solely for your business, including a business phone line, web hosting, etc.

When you work for yourself, this means that you are also responsible for purchasing your own health insurance. As such, health insurance is a potential deduction for anyone who has to purchase their own coverage, including those who are self-employed.

If you write a book and plan to later travel for seminars, speaking engagements and/or consulting services, you may be able to deduct travel expenses, including those related to your car or truck. Related deductions might also include auto repairs, insurance, gasoline, mileage, depreciation and other factors that relate directly to the business use of your automobile.

If you travel, you may also be able to deduct the cost of your accommodations and/or meals.

As we all know, advertising is a large expense for any business. As such, self-employed individuals can deduct the cost of advertising, legal services, interest, real estate mortgage and taxes related to business assets, etc. You should check with your tax advisor for specifics, but you will almost certainly be pleasantly surprised.

Now that you know what to deduct, it's important to know how to properly claim your expenses. Always retain a copy of receipts and, if possible, keep them all in one place for easy retrieval. This will serve as your records, proof of purchase and will help you to calculate any deductions quickly and easily.

Reason 40

Improved Lifestyle

A friend of mine works in personal security for many famous people when they come to town. The person that he enjoyed the most was the Dalai Lama last time he came to town. He personally gave my friend a scarf and a small book that I had the honor of reading.

The pivotal point of this book was his answer for the purpose of life. Doesn't everyone want to know the purpose of life? I know I sure did. Well here is his answer. 'Happiness' The purpose of life is happiness. I agree one hundred percent, because nothing else really matters if you don't have happiness.

Happiness is a choice and is something that is an "inside job" for all of us. Happiness will magically attract to you all you want and need to have to be successful and abundant and not the other way around. If you are not happy now, then you won't be happy when you are rich either.

Choose happiness and choose an improved lifestyle. What does the Dalai Lama, improved lifestyle and writing a book have to do with each other? Because writing and publishing a book is the same process. You choose what you want to write about and create it from the inside out just like happiness.

The writing of your book puts you in touch with your inner creative being where you choose the outcome you want and most will choose a much improved lifestyle. When you have happiness and creativity all working in harmony within yourself, you will attract the wondrous life of your dreams

Reason 41

Creates More Value

Do you want the secret to getting very rich? Always give more value than what your customers are paying for. I think it is Zig Ziglar who says if you help enough people get what they want, you will get what you want. Give value in any of your books and you will have the formula for amazing success.

Whatever it is that you want, give it away. If you want a better life and more money then give your customers good information on how they can have a better life and more money. All this information is available to all of us just be the conduit for spreading the word. It is an ever expanding universe.

Just the process of writing and expressing your thoughts are adding to the world's value. If you write your truth from your heart you will automatically be adding immense value for many people.

Always look at your book as something that will be of value to your reader. If you follow this simple formula, then you are guaranteed success.

Reason 42

Increased Focus

One of the key ingredients I have noticed about really successful people is how focused they are. They don't try to do everything all at once, they just focus on one thing at a time until they have mastered it and then they move on to the next task.

Your path to success will start with a single focus and that will be to write your book. It will be easy for you with the simple systems we have later on in this book to accomplish it in a very short time. With a single focus on your book, you should be able to write and publish your book in about 40 days.

When you hold a magnifying glass at the right angle over a piece of paper you can direct the sun's rays to focus on one spot that will ignite the piece of paper. You will be practicing the same thing when you focus your thoughts on the one goal of writing your book.

Writing your book will easily help you focus on each step one at a time for the further information products that you will need for your customers as you further grow your book business on its road to success.

Believe it or not, it can sometimes be difficult to focus on just one thing. This is especially true when you are trying to start your own business.

Writing a book will increase your focus and force you to concentrate on your specialty. Knowledge is the key to success and it's when you tap into that inner being of intelligence that you are rewarded with a better more prosperous life.

Reason 43

Higher Consciousness

Everything you need or want in life you already have even if you are not aware of it yet. As Bob Proctor says, the only difference between a man that makes $50,000 per year and the man that makes $500,000 per year is that the $50,000 man is not aware of the fact he can make more money.

You can never hear anything above your level of consciousness. If you are not an auto mechanic, then you will not understand what an auto mechanic is talking about until you raise your awareness or consciousness and learn some information about auto mechanics.

The more you raise your awareness the more things you have available to you because now you see or hear the information you could not once understand. What does this have to do with writing your book?

You, by the nature of going through the process of writing, will be continually raising your consciousness level and become aware of the things that are available to you. When you are conscious of something, you are aware of it. If you want to heighten your awareness within your career, there's no better way of doing so than to author a book.

When you research, compile and write a book, you will learn a lot. It's plain and simple. Knowledge is like happiness; you can never have too much. As an author you will thrive in being even more knowledgeable about your book topic and the hours that you spend completing your work will raise your awareness of the subject in a way that few others could ever compete with.

Reason 44

You Will Be Taken More Seriously

When you are the expert in your field people listen. You don't go to a janitor and ask for medical advice you go to a Doctor because they are perceived as the expert. The Doctor's expertise was accomplished by years of schooling to get their medical degree and now we, as the general public, take their advice more seriously because they are the experts.

It is no different in any other vocation; we take expert's advice more seriously. The nice thing about writing your book is you don't have to pay tens of thousands of dollars and study for years to be perceived as the expert. Write a book and you are there.

In fact, I know of a very renowned Doctor of Psychology that studied hard for years. She said her income and professional stature shot up only after she wrote a book. Many people have a hard time believing this because they are so used to having to struggle to get everything they have.

If they don't struggle for what they have many will sabotage the results and won't believe it. But it is true that more often then not a book will trump your credentials and propel you further ahead in life because people take you more seriously.

Most people take authors more seriously than the very people that have studied a topic. It may not be right, but it is very real and I am passionate when I say you must write a book.

Reason 45

Easier To Up Sell Existing Customers

Once you have a relationship with your customers they will be three times more likely to buy from you than a completely new customer. Your present customers are not only more likely to buy they are also easier to deal with and a lot more profitable because you have already paid the acquisition cost to acquire that customer.

When someone has bought or read your book they are automatically adding themselves to your list as a customer. You don't have to go through the process of proving who you are and selling them something because they have already bought and read your book.

People buy more often and at a higher price from people they trust. You are quickly and simply short circuiting the trust factor time line by writing your book. Your sales per customer list will be extremely profitable and if done properly can be as simple as making money on demand.

Anytime you have more information of good value to your list and you already know that this is the information that will help them with a problem and give them excellent value, you only have to let your customers know about it and they are likely to buy it.

Reason 46

Attracts The Guys

Okay, girls, lets have some fun here. I don't think it is any secret that your celebrity as an author can have some pretty strong attraction power for attracting some pretty interesting male dating material. We are a celebrity obsessed society and it is time to have fun with your new found celebrity.

Maybe before you had not attracted that mega successful business man or that sports star. Play with where your book will take you and be open to new opportunities in the dating world.

Your book will open you up to events you may have not normally have had access to, so take advantage and go have fun.

Reason 47

Attracts The Girls

There is nothing more attractive than an intelligent man, so don't be afraid to let your knowledge be known. If you want to attract the woman of your dreams, show her that you're smart and ambitious.

Imagine yourself at a seminar or a book signing. Everyone present will be there to see you, so don't be surprised if you meet someone special. They say that it's possible to meet people in the strangest of places, so keep an open eye and mind when it comes to romance.

In addition to being one of the most popular marketing tools, having written your own book is just as good as having a magnet that draws people in, and you never know who that next person may be.

Reason 48

A Book Is A Valuable Sales Tool

A book as a sales tool blows many other advertising options out of the water. When you think about traditional marketing techniques, what comes to mind? Print advertisements, commercials and internet promotions? Each of these methods has potential, but they all have one thing in common. They can cost you a fortune and there aren't any guarantees that they will help to increase your sales.

As the author of a book, you are actually earning money from your sales tool. When people buy your book, you earn money. When they read it and decide to purchase more products or services from you, you earn money. Do you see the recurring theme here? It's money and your book is the key to unlocking the wealth that you deserve.

How will your book be a valuable sales tool? First and foremost, it makes others think of you as an expert, which is a very valuable title to have when it comes to marketing your product or service. Secondly, a book gives customers the chance to see what you're made of before spending a lot of money.

Think about it this way. If you were searching for a consultant, would you rather spend thousands of dollars upfront to hire someone you hadn't heard of before or would you prefer to deal with someone that had written a book on the topic and made you feel educated after having read it?

Customers will want to do business with you because they will trust you. It's just that simple. If you write an informative, smart and well-researched book, people will know it and they will come to you for additional products.

Reason 49

People Will Want To Do
Business With You

People like doing business with people they like. I mean, how
often will you go to do business with someone you don't like?
Never! Why do you like to shop in your favorite grocery store?
What makes you want to go back every week? Is it their pricing,
their availability or the fact that they have been around for
awhile and you trust them to have what you need?

It doesn't matter what type of business you are running.
Customers are your main concern and, as such, you want them
to want you. Your book will be a strong attractor for drawing
customers to you.

Writing a book will make people want to do business with
you. If they want to spend their time and money on an industry
expert with the experience and knowledge to back it up, they
will look to you.

Reason 50

Reciprocity Power

When you give something to someone it is very hard for that
person to not respond in like kind. A few years ago I was in the
San Fransisco Airport looking rather lost when someone behind
a counter asked me if he could help me? I asked if he knew
where Gate 12 was and he quickly gave me directions.

What happened next was one of the most powerful laws

I know of for getting people to respond to you in kind. Right after he finished helping me with directions he pulled a binder out from under the counter and explained he was raising money for homeless children and would appreciate if I could help with a financial donation.

It would take a very strong person to say no and not hand over some money to help the charity. I had been "set up" by the Law of Reciprocity, and it worked. Had he just asked for a donation and not given me the directions it would have been much easier for me to say no and he knew that.

As the author of your book you are giving first and by giving value and help you are triggering this powerful Law of Reciprocity. Anytime you're asking for help or a sale in the future your customer's resistance to saying no has been diminished substantially by this law and will bring to you much abundance.

Reason 51

You Will Get Media Attention

Who gets media attention? Celebrities, right? As an author, you are a celebrity. Experts? As an author, you are perceived as an expert. Those participating in newsworthy events? As an author, your book is the newsworthy event. Some people like media attention and some don't, but as an author, the media can be a very valuable marketing venue.

From newspapers to trade magazines, television and radio shows, you are likely to find an easy road to free publicity if you market yourself and your book properly. All it takes is sending a free copy of your new book and a press kit to the necessary media outlets. In most cases, you will be amazed by the attention you are getting from both the media and your customers.

Reason 52

Create Your Own Luck

Luck is preparation meeting opportunity. In other words, you create your own luck. The day you start writing your book you will be well down the path to creating your own luck and lots of it.

Anyone who is successful today has put all the building blocks in place to create that luck. If you think that having a good income and being successful is something that only lucky people get in life then you are indeed in luck today.

You will create unlimited opportunities for money, travel, fame and more when you market and position yourself after you have written and published your book. You don't need years of schooling, tons of money or even certified credentials to create your own luck from writing a book.

Do you believe in chance or do you, like many, feel that you have control over your own destiny? The decisions that you make will ultimately determine the kind of luck that you have. When you make the decision to write a book, you are essentially saying that you believe in yourself and your talents. In fact, you believe in them so much that you are taking a big leap, putting yourself out there and opening your mind up to the idea that people around the world will have access to your book. Yes, your book. Your thoughts. Your words and, more importantly, your work.

Most people will agree that there are two types of

entrepreneurs in this world. There are those who think about what they want to do and there are those who get out there and do it. When it comes to business, there's really no in between. There's no gray area. If you are ready to take control over your own destiny, luck and future, put your thoughts onto paper and use them to create a book.

Reason 53

Interviews By Publication

(magazines, newspapers, etc.)

Every interview you do increases your expert status and credibility. Writing your book will bring more fame by interviews. The next time you are at a newsstand, pick up a magazine. I am certain that you will see an interview of some type inside the issue. When your local newspaper arrives, flip through it and look for a story about accomplishment. As an author, you may just find yourself the subject of the next big story.

As a writer myself, I can tell you that magazine editors are always on the lookout for a good story. They look for interviews, feature stories and anything newsworthy relating to their genre. If you are a weight loss expert who just so happens to have written a new book on the topic, magazine editors may be interested in featuring your story. How did you become a writer? What do you hope to accomplish with your latest book? Will there be future editions? These are all common questions that a magazine editor will love to have you answer.

In much the same fashion, newspaper editors are looking for that special hometown story that lets readers know what their local notable is up to.

If you are an author, you can get a lot of coverage simply by submitting a press release to the editor of local and state newspapers. They may not only publish your news, but they may also contact you for an interview.

In addition to these opportunities being very rewarding, they also offer valuable publicity for both you and your book. Being featured in a magazine or newspaper is an accomplishment in its own right, and every author knows that this type of publicity is one of the best.

Reason 54

Interviews By Radio

Talk radio continues to grow in North America and being interviewed as an author makes great radio content. People love to listen to the expert espouse their knowledge and learn a new trick or tip themselves. How often do you listen to the radio? When you are tuning in, do you ever notice special guests that are either in studio or call in for a telephone interview? If you listen to the radio, especially during the morning, you have likely heard both.

Radio stations are a form of entertainment, but they are also very much a part of the media world. They forecast weather, promote upcoming events and, more importantly, talk about the latest news. As the author of your book, you will be the news. Getting yourself some air time is not a difficult task, especially if the show host views you as an expert and your topic is especially interesting.

Much like print media, radio publicity is a very positive

reflection of you as an author and the quality of your work. In most cases, the host will make a comment about your book or ask you to talk about it in some way. When you think about it, a radio interview is like a free commercial with credibility. It's easy to purchase airtime for a commercial, but it takes an expert to be interviewed live on the air.

Reason 55

Interviews By Television

Let's face the facts. You are a hundred times more likely to end up on a TV show if you are an author or expert. TV producers demand and get the best people for their shows and you will already have positioned yourself as the expert by writing your book.

When it comes to publicity, don't be surprised if you're invited to participate in a live televised interview. You could be featured on a local television news broadcast or, if your book and work become more popular, you may even end up on a national show.

When you appear on television, you are taking your work to a whole new level. You're going beyond print media and putting a face and voice with your name. People will see and hear you. If you are able to spark their interest, they are more likely to try your product or service in the future.

Reason 56

Builds Momentum In Your Business

Not only does writing your book build momentum for your business, your book will also be a hard-working good will ambassador for your business for many years to come. Your book will be out there diligently working for you 24 hours a day, 7 days a week, quietly creating more momentum by each person who is introduced to your book.

In order for your business to keep moving forward, you have to pace yourself in such a way that success is possible. Momentum is the speed at which you set that pace and it will play a large role in the betterment of your business.

When you write a book, forward movement is automatically created. As you achieve something new, it will reflect on your business. Writing a book, my friend, is very good momentum to have. As is the case with all things in life, you have to keep moving if you expect to get anywhere. After all, how far would your car go if your foot wasn't on the gas pedal? Don't let your life or career slip into neutral. Build momentum in your business and do it by writing a book.

Reason 57

Builds Momentum In Your Life

I don't think anyone would debate the positive impact that writing your own book would have on your life, especially when it comes to momentum. Much like the way you hope to build momentum in your business, moving forward in life is important for both personal and financial fulfillment.

On a personal note, writing a book is good for your soul. It will make you feel proud in your accomplishment, eager to see what the future holds and you will never again be afraid to go for your dreams. When you see that first book published with your name on it, you will feel as though you have just hit the jackpot.

Life is about moving forward. It's about setting goals and living your passion to reach them. Business reasons aside, accomplishing your goals will build momentum in your life.

Reason 58

Writing Is Thinking Put Into Action

Everything you see in your world began with a thought. Plain and simple is the fact that thoughts become things. Whether it was the printing press or the airplane, it was a thought first before it was brought into the physical world. Thoughts are the seeds and the action you take with those thoughts can change the world for generations to come.

When you write your book you are taking your thought seeds and turning them into something physical that will add value to the world, now and in the future. It is such a simple concept with such dramatic power, that we all have and must take this great opportunity

It's easy enough to think about doing something, but it's an entirely new ball game when you make the decision to do it. When you write a book, you are putting your thoughts into words. They are no longer just random ideas floating in and out of your mind. Your words will now have the opportunity to inspire, educate and help others in a way that only your uniqueness can.

When you think about writing a book, you are planning to put your ideas into motion. When you put your pen to paper or your fingers to the keyboard and begin to write that first book, you are putting your mind into motion. That motion or action creates a physical book to be enjoyed for many years to come.

Reason 59

Attracts Like-Minded People To You

The simplest definition of The Law Of Attraction states that 'Like Attracts Like.' By simple definition then, your authoring a book about a specific topic will attract more like minded people to you that are interested in your topic.

To attract and network with others means to interact or exchange information and develop contacts. When it comes to the world of business, who you know can be as important as what you know. When you have the ability to attract and network with individuals who think like you or are on the same career path, you will experience a whole new ever expanding world of opportunities.

I'll give you an example. Think about some of your favorite internet haunts. Why do you like them? Is it because you can meet people who share your interests or whom you have a bond with?

Perhaps you frequent a website designed to reconnect you with former high school classmates or a message board where you can discuss career, education or other hobbies and interests. Whatever the case, we all enjoy being around those with whom we can talk and share similar interests.

The above scenario is a good example of social networking,

but it's worth noting that business networking isn't so different. When you network socially, you do so for fun. In business, you do so to make connections and develop bonds with other professionals in your industry.

This could lead to future career projects, greater opportunities, referrals, etc. The possibilities are practically endless because business contacts really can make a difference in your life.

Networking with like-minded professionals, can and likely will, play a significant role in your profession. In addition to inspiring you to achieve goals, it will also help to improve communication and will most likely help you to improve your problem-solving skills.

Whether you network for business or pleasure, meeting those with whom you share like mindedness can be extremely beneficial. Thanks to the internet, you now have a whole new world of opportunities to attract colleagues and other industry professionals who you may otherwise never know. Creativity abounds when great minds get together, which is why networking may give your career a big boost.

Reason 60

Challenges You To Move Forward

The first step can be the hardest to take, but once you have done it you put into force a momentum that will carry you even further. Writing your book will kick start you to constantly propel yourself forward. You will naturally attract other opportunities that you will want to act on.

Have you ever heard someone say that despite their past achievements, they always want more? When you become an author, you will be challenged to move forward and keep doing more to further your career.

When you write one book, and learn how easy it really is to accomplish you will probably start thinking about your next book and so forth. It's human nature. In challenging yourself to move forward, you are simply demanding nothing less than progress.

Reason 61

Writing A Book Exercises Your Brain

You are either growing or dying! Exercising your brain is one of the best ways to keep yourself young. Think of your brain as you would the rest of your body. Does it need exercise every day in order to stay fit and healthy? Yes. Will your muscles weaken without it? Yes.

When you write, you are giving your brain a workout. You are thinking, pondering, creating ideas in your head and then figuring out a way to put them onto paper in such a way that will make sense to your readers.

Just as you would care for your body, make sure that you keep your mind moving and challenged on a daily basis. Through these exercises, you will gain even more strength and brainpower.

Reason 62

Gives You A Sense Of Accomplishment

I can tell you from my own experience that the writing of a book has given me one of my greatest senses of accomplishments. From having thoughts, to putting them on paper, to being published, your book really does take on a life of its own. It is a document of work that will be enjoyed by readers for years to come, maybe decades.

When you write a book, you will feel a great sense of achievement because you are an author. This is a title that will stay with you for the rest of your life. It's not a job title; it's a permanent title. When you work for someone, you may have earned a certain job title within the company. But what happens when you no longer work for that company or change careers altogether? You no longer have the right to refer to yourself using an old job title. But, as an author, you will always carry that accomplishment with you.

Although writing a book can be a simple task, as we will show you later in this book, most people believe it is not a simple thing. They think it takes time, intelligence, dedication, and a passion for the work that you do. There is nothing better than starting a project and sticking with it until completion.

This alone will give you a sense of accomplishment. But when you hold the book that you have written in your hand for the first time, gaze at the glossy cover and see your name on the title page, nothing that I can tell you here will compare to the sense of pride and accomplishment that you will feel.

Reason 63

You Will Become More Popular

Just by the mere exercise of authoring a book, you will be putting out to the universe yourself as the attractive character that wrote the book. Authors are popular just by the very nature of what they do. People want to read your book and know you, and that is popularity.

Although most of your readers may think they know you, and the fact of the matter is that most will not. Most of your readers will have a perceived idea of who you are and will be drawn to those character traits although it will be made up in their own minds. You are popular because they made you popular by the very things your readers have imagined about you. By the very nature of the publishing world, you will become more popular when you write a book.

If you want to be the life of the party, the person that everyone wants to talk to and the one who all others want to know, then write a book. You will gain popularity, respect, and most of all great pride in the work that you do.

Reason 64

Writing A Book Can Help You

Conquer Fears

Almost 85% of the population of North America operates in the "fear and anger" consciousness mode. When you operate in fear you don't make good decisions in your life and you also attract the very things you don't want. Once you have gone through the process of writing your book you will have conquered any fears you previously had about writing and that will spill over into other areas of your life.

Once you have conquered the writing of a book you will easily move from fear and anger to love and happiness. You will be in the top 15% of our population who are making good life decisions based on love and happiness, and attracting all the benefits of life by making much better decisions.

An author is someone who isn't afraid to accomplish what they set out to do. Yes, there may be some anxiety in the beginning, but that fear is quickly overcome with determination. When this happens, you will begin to carry this trait over into your everyday life. It may start out slowly at first, but it will begin to grow.

You won't be afraid to set goals for yourself, seek out the best way to accomplish them and see them through to completion. As you progress as an author, you will overcome fears associated with writing and in everyday life. You will come to know what your work is worth and you will refuse to accept anything less.

Reason 65

Builds Inner Strength

Inner strength is accomplished by completing any worthwhile task and one of the best is to write a book. To take your book from thought right through to publication is an accomplishment that is of serious magnitude in many people's eyes. It can quite often be a solitary mission being the author of your own book and is a journey of building inner strength.

Inner strength is something that is needed as you grow

your book business, and you acquire it in spades during the process of writing. You will easily move to other information products that you can up sell in addition to your books once you have developed that inner strength.

Each step you take along the journey in your business will become much easier because you will have developed your valuable inner strength to easily carry you through all obstacles. The creative component of being an author will give you everything you need to carry you through the evolving inner strength you will now have.

Reason 66

Makes You Dream Bigger

Here is a fascinating stat! Eighty one percent of our population believes they have a book inside of them but very few will realize their dream of writing a book. It is such a tragedy because once you finish your book and see the opportunities that come to you your dreams will become much bigger.

After you have written your book, and continue to stay in touch with others who have gone through the same process, you will be introduced to all sorts of dreams bigger than you could have ever imagined before you wrote your book. You will find that one opportunity will lead to the next, and the next, with each dream being bigger than the last.

You will have opportunities from both like-minded people you attract through your book, as well as the opportunities of the authors that will help you to see the bigger opportunities that have been presented to them. You of course will also have all the media-related opportunities that can spin off to any number of the unseen dreams not available in the past.

As an author you are only limited by your own mind to

dream big. You will find that by the virtues of author hood that big dreams will present themselves in many ways to you if you are open to receiving.

Reason 67

Changes Your Paradigm

Writing your book will break you free of your old paradigm. Many people live today exactly as they did yesterday and the day before. Once you have written and published your book you will be forced to change your old paradigm because of the many different life and business opportunities that will be presented to you.

It will be like taking a new route to work because you never know who you will run into and what new circumstances will come your way. Your book may create new pathways that will present other circumstances each and every time someone new reads your book.

You are forced to break free of your old way of thinking, because you have new information out in the universe through your book that is working for you around the clock. You may be asked to attend new situations and events that will forever more shake up the hard-to-die old paradigm.

Reason 68

You Can Accomplish More Through A Book

There is no doubt that you can accomplish a lot more through a book especially in the marketing world. Your book can be available through your website, book stores, libraries, seminars etc. The ways to market your book are virtually endless.

Once your book is made available through all the different marketing venues, it will then be doing its job of accomplishing its purpose in your customer's hands. Once it's in your customers hands it does the personal public relations work each time it is read. Your book will also attract new customers to you because you're the expert with the credibility they are looking for.

You can not buy this type of advertising through traditional methods such as ads in the paper, flyers, radio etc. Your book will be like a third party blowing your own horn without you doing it. The power of the credibility you gain as a publish author is perceived as an endorsement by many of your future customers.

You will be able to accomplish much more, and in less time, with the expert status and credibility that your book will bring you. Not only can your book make your customers less price resistant but it can also be a lot easier to charge a premium price. You will attract more customers, at premium prices, which will make you be able to accomplish a lot more through our book.

Reason 69

Your Kids Will Get Excited

I remember when I mentioned to my middle daughter Lex that I was writing a book she was very interested. She asked me what it was about and would she be in the book. It was a month or so later that I realized how excited she really was because she regularly asked how my book was coming along.

I think it shows even in your children's world the title of author means something. Lex was obviously excited and proud that her Dad was authoring a book. It was almost a little embarrassing when Lex would tell all the waiters at a restaurant that her Dad is writing a book!

I am sure your kids will want you to give a little talk in their class and the goodwill of authoring a book will spread throughout your kid's friends by example. So the moral of this story is make your kids proud and probably your kid's will author a book one day as well. Remember: like daughter, like father.

By the way you have to do this before your children one day realize that you aren't actually God.

Reason 70

Your Parents Will Be Proud Of You

How many times have your parents told you that they would be proud of you, no matter what you did? This is how most parents feel about their children and they probably never hesitate to tell you. However, no parent could deny the extra

glimmer of pride that they have for their child who works hard to achieve
success.

When you write a book, even the parent who often struggles with showing their emotions will be overcome with pride. We all know someone who has trouble expressing their feelings, but there is no doubt that mom and dad will soon be bragging about you to their friends, colleagues and your other relatives. Your success is a reflection of their parenting and will be a wonderful way to celebrate the family name.

Reason 71

Opens Doors

What do you hope to achieve in life? If you are reading this book, you are obviously searching for something more. When you write your own book, you will open doors that you never even thought possible. In addition to becoming an expert, and possibly adding to your business a consulting and/or public speaking career, you may enjoy the thrill of seeing your name in the media.

When you become an author, be ready for the attention that comes with the job. You may get offers from magazines, newspapers, television and radio shows to be interviewed. After becoming an author, you will find a marked increase in your business by virtue of the many different doors that will now be open to you.

Holding your own book in hand is as good as the key to an unlocked door. What's behind the door? Your future, of course. So, why keep it waiting? Unlock the key to your potential and enjoy the road to success. You've earned it!

Reason 72

Working Outside The Box

Thinking outside the box is one thing, but working outside the box will present you with a whole new ball game. What does it mean? Simply put, this implies that you are doing something different, creative, imaginative, and unique.

Writing and publishing your book gives you an opportunity to attract business to you in a whole new way. No more of the labor intensive "push model" for sales, instead you will be using the "pull model." You don't have to go out and get sales, rather you will attract people who want to do business with you and buy what you have to sell.

Your book is by far the best way on the planet to work outside the box. The more you discover and develop what will be attracted and available to you, the more ideas and opportunities will be presented. If you are open to new possibilities of working outside the box you will see you business grow exponentially with unlimited options. Many options will be revealed to you later in this book but they are truly limitless.

An author is someone who takes charge, a leader and someone who is regarded with great respect. Let's face it. Being an author is not a common thing. Not everyone that you meet will have the honor of telling you they have published a book.

You will know this is true when you, yourself, tell people that you have written a book. In most cases, you will get a 'wow' response. Don't be surprised if you get a few who even look at you with disbelief. It's nothing personal; being an author is just not your average, everyday accomplishment.

When you work for yourself, create new opportunities and go the extra mile to live life the way that you want to live it, you are thinking and working outside the box. But hey, you have a much better view and there's always a lot more freedom when you find yourself venturing outside of the box.

Reason 73

Helps People To Remember You

If you are sincerely interested in the person you are talking to, then they will be interested in you. Ask a few questions and listen to them talk and you will be a home run that people will remember.

Whether you are introduced as an author or mention that you are an author it will be an amazing starting point that people will remember you by. First of all, there are still not a lot of authors relative to the population so being introduced as an author makes people remember you.

Remember that you can use your book as your business card when you get the opportunity to. People will always remember the person who gives them their book as opposed to the traditional business card. Don't be shy in utilizing your opportunity to be remembered because the more people that remember you the stronger your brand will be.

Reason 74

For Posterity

As an author, you will be paving the way for future generations to earn an amazing living by working for themselves. Today, more and more people are choosing to work at home instead of the typical 9 to 5 job. The more success that we earn today, the better chance those future generations will enjoy the same luxuries, with the possibility of even more benefits.

Not so long ago, anyone who was not self-employed was required to show up at the office, clock in and fall into the typical daily rut. Now, some employers are allowing their employees to work out of their home.

This is just an example of how the world is changing and, as an author, public speaker and consultant; you will have the opportunity to continue making changes that will affect the future of our children, grandchildren and so on.

Reason 75

Free Publicity

Everyone likes freebies, especially when it comes to publicity. It doesn't matter whether you are just starting a new business or are simply operating one that's on a budget, you will enjoy having one of the largest expenses that many businesses face being reduced down to practically nothing.

As an author, especially if you self-publish, you will be responsible for most if not all of the publicity surrounding your book. Do you know the cost of running a print ad, buying radio airtime or purchasing a 30-second television commercial? These can be overwhelming, which is why advertising costs are some of the greatest budget busters for any business.

Later in this book, we will show you how getting publicity for your book and your business is as easy as picking up the phone, mailing an envelope or sending an e-mail. A press release remains the most popular way to gain free publicity for a book. After all, customers have to know about your book before they can purchase it and the media can help to get the word out quickly and cheaply. If you want to maximize your media potential, make sure to submit your press release to newspaper and magazine editors, radio and television talk show hosts, and press release distribution websites.

As an author, you should get a personalized website that will attract customers to opt-in to your mailing list. Promoting your website on the web is another popular avenue for attracting customers. Search engine ranking, article marketing, press releases and business cards can all help to drive website traffic to you and continually build your business.

Reason 76

Writing One Book Can Lead To Another Book

Once you write your first book and realize how easy it can be you will find your next book will be almost an automatic response to information you want to further get out to your audience. You will gain momentum once you have written your first book.

Joe Vitale is a marketing genius that uses the phrase "Author Of Too Many Books To List," to describe himself. He has the momentum second to none to write good books and use them as a constant source of publicity. Like Joe, each book you write will become easier than the book before and your collection of books will build rapidly if you so choose.

Don't forget that as you build your customer list, it is only natural that if they liked your first book, a number of them will automatically buy your second book. It is always easier to market to your current customers than it is to find and acquire new customers.

Reason 77

You Will Have The Ability To Touch People's Lives

If you are able to help your reader in some way through a life experience you have had, then you can really communicate with and touch that reader. Do you know what it feels like to help someone? I mean, really help someone. What if you could produce a work that significantly touched the lives of your readers? If someone has a problem, wouldn't you want to help them? As a writer, you have the ability to touch others through your words and your knowledge.

Imagine if you were to write a practical how-to book on getting out of debt. Now we all know that someone in debt probably doesn't have a lot of extra money to spend, but perhaps they are looking for an answer that will help them to regain control over their lives. Suppose they look to you for that answer and using their money, which isn't plentiful, they take a risk and purchase your book.

Now suppose these same individuals use the strategies noted in your book to legally and ethically get themselves out of debt. Do you know how significant this is? The information that you provided could literally give someone a new start in life.

Tell me this: In what other way could you possibly reach out and help these individuals? How would you ever come to know them or their situation? How would they know you? As an author, your book is available around the world and you can reach people that you would otherwise never even know.

In helping others, you will feel good in knowing that you are changing lives one reader at a time.

Reason 78

Set Yourself Apart

As an expert, an author and a professional in your field, you will be setting yourself apart from others in your vocation. You have built credibility and expertise with your book and separated yourself from any of your competitors.

When people have questions or are in need of an expert, they will come to you first. Why? Because you are the author. You're the expert and they believe that you will be able to provide them with the best and most informative information.

For instance, if you are in the field of business and are particularly knowledgeable in the area of investments, you aren't alone. But what makes the information that you have to share so much more valuable than that of your competition? The truth is that nobody will know unless you show them. And what's the best way to show them? Write a book and let your penned words speak for themselves. When you do this, you are not only sharing your knowledge with the world, but you are doing so in a positive way that says "hey, look at me! Here I am and this is what I know."

How many of your competitors have taken such a gamble on themselves and their talent? It's one thing to sit behind an office desk and quietly consult with a customer here and there, but how much confidence will it take to show the world what you are made of? When you write a book, you are demonstrating that confidence and others will be drawn to you because of it. If you really want to set yourself apart, learn to showcase the 3 P's of professionalism: potential, pride and personable.

Reason 79

Builds Your Name

Most people don't realize the importance of their name because most don't think of the credibility they have behind their name. What is a name? It's a word by which you are known. It can also signify your reputation. When you write a book, your name will be on the front cover, the inside cover, the back cover and you will forever be known as the person responsible for this magnificent achievement.

In addition to being a valuable marketing tool, your book will add a great deal of pride to your name. As you sit quietly, say your full name to yourself. It's your given name and it's cherished, right? Now, imagine introducing yourself to another for the first time at a seminar or speaking engagement. Imagine yourself extending your hand and saying, "Hello. My name is John Smith and I'm the author." Doesn't that have a nice ring to it? You bet it does!

When your name is on file with the Library of Congress, the U.S. Copyright Office, thousands of internet websites, both online and traditional bookstores and is often seen in print publications, your name is out there. You have 'made it' as an author and it's all because you took the first step and wrote a book.

Reason 80

Create Customer Traffic

Your book will have the potential to create a steady stream of customer traffic. In addition to book lovers who are simply interested in your topic, you will also attract potential customers who may be interested in purchasing a product or service that you may be offering, hiring you as a speaker or as a consultant.

Traffic can be created through your book in many different ways and we will cover many of them in this book. Book stores, websites, E-zines, customer lists, joint ventures the way you attract customer traffic is indeed endless. You will always have new and innovative ways to attract customer traffic through your book.

A book is an amazing tool. It has the ability to attract people from many angles, but the key is how far your book will actually reach. As an author, customers are not restricted to your local area, state or even country. When your title is published and offered online through major book retailers, you may attract customers across the globe.

So, what happens next? Those who read your book will tell their friends, family and business colleagues. As the word begins to spread, you will have the potential to generate even more traffic.

Reason 81

Create Fans

The nature of the business of book writing says you will automatically create fans. A fan of course is someone who loves you, your work or that which you stand for. Do you have a favorite music group, singer, actress or actor? If you are like most people, you are a fan of someone or something. Perhaps it's a television show, movie or sport. Whatever the case, we all have our favorites and we adore them. They become a part of our lives and have the ability to entertain us in some way.

As an author, you will have fans who will also be grateful for your help if you have written a non fiction "How To" book. It's just that simple. People will read your book; they will want to see more of your work and don't be surprised if you even get a few autograph requests. The truth is that authors are famous and fans are just an added benefit.

Reason 82

You Will Have A Stronger Life Purpose

If someone walked up to you right now and asked what your purpose is in life, what would you say? What is the driving force behind your greatest resolve or determination? If you don't know, then it's time to make a decision. Are you ready to change your life? Are you prepared to be in a position to change the lives of others?

As an author, you are not only making a difference in your life as a writer. Your words can also change the lives of others and this is an important purpose that can give you the greatest determination of all.

It's important to have goals, something that you can work toward and achieve. When you set out on a journey, isn't the whole point of the trip to get to the destination? Your life is a journey and it's how you proceed that makes the difference. As a goal-oriented individual, you will work harder and you will be more focused on your achievement. When you have a strong purpose in life, you will be inspired to accomplish anything that you set your mind to.

Reason 83

Makes You Immortal

Your book can live forever and you are the soul of your book. How neat is that? Now that so much information is being logged on the internet you will naturally be a part of history through your book. By definition, immortal means to live forever. But it also means deserving of being remembered eternally and/or a person of enduring fame. When you write a book, your name will live on forever through your work.

But writing a book is much more than just being remembered. It's about a celebration of your dedication and knowledge surrounding a specific topic. As an author, you will enjoy enduring fame.

Have you ever met someone who feels lost or expresses their concern that they have yet to leave their 'mark' on the world? I think we all know someone like that, but this is your chance to leave a legacy that will forever be remembered and celebrated by future generations.

If you want to be remembered for an eternity, now is the time to start making a difference. Write a book that will change the world or, at the very least, the lives of some of the people who live in it.

Reason 84

You Can Live Anywhere

This is one of the most important aspects for me writing a book. I have been successful in a "brick and mortar" for over 3 decades and it was time for a major change in my life. I wanted out of the daily life of more customers, more trucks, and more employees. I found I did not enjoy it as much as I did when I was a little younger, although the money was still very good.

The good money can trap you if you are not careful. For me, it really didn't matter how much money I could make from my brick and mortar business, because it could never be enough to hold me back from making a major life change.

The aspect of becoming an author was very attractive for a few reasons. The first is I can do it until the day I die because I can't imagine waking up in the morning without some way of adding value to our world. The second reason is that I can have a very successful book and information marketing business operate from anywhere in the world. That is extremely exciting to me.

How would you like to wake up to a Hawaiian sunrise? Or perhaps you prefer an ocean breeze kissing your face on a warm Florida evening, a snow-capped mountain view in Colorado or a beautiful autumn afternoon in Vermont. Whatever your pleasure, it can be yours.

As an author, your location is no longer defined by your work. Instead of you having to move for a job, your career will go with you anywhere. Just imagine the freedom of being able to live anywhere that you want without having to worry about the local employment opportunities.

Many people dream of a quiet, serene country home nestled on privately wooded acres without a neighbor in sight. The only problem with this is that there aren't a lot of job opportunities in the country. Although beautiful, it's not exactly the employment haven that you would get in the city. When you become a successful author, none of this matters anymore. Live where you want, work at home and enjoy whatever view you choose from your front door.

Reason 85

Creates Passive Income

I have enjoyed passive income since I was a 12 year old. I was the business kid in the neighborhood that instead of delivering papers myself I had several paper routes and sub contracted them to other kids in the neighborhood. I would collect the money from my subs each Friday and split the profits with them and never deliver a paper.

If you have passive income, you are basically earning money without having to put forth any significant action. Yes, you wrote the book. But this same book that took you a month to write could earn you money for a lifetime. Aside from future sales and royalties, a book has the ability to produce a steady cash flow for your business through the sale of information products or services.

Your book can sell at anytime, day or night, weekdays, weekends and even holidays. If your title is listed with online bookstores, you can even earn money while you sleep. If you use your book as a marketing tool, your business can earn customers and sales without you having to continually advertise your company. Why? Because your book is a powerful marketing tool on its own.

Reason 86

People Need To Hear Your Unique Message

Most people don't realize this truth but we all have a unique message to give to the world. We all have a different way of seeing and doing things and they are all important to share with each other.

What do you have to offer the world? You obviously have an idea for a book floating around in your mind or perhaps you have a manuscript that you wrote years ago sitting around collecting dust. Why? People need to hear what you have to say and, if your book can help them, you need to publish it.

Think about all of the books that are out there and what they have to say. Is every one helpful? No. Can yours be helpful in some way? If the answer is yes, do yourself and the public a favor by showing what you have to offer. Educating your readers with your own unique message will give both you and them satisfaction.

Reason 87

Your Book Is An Extension Of You

Who is writing your new book? You. Who thought of the idea? You. Who will be reaping the benefits? You. Do you see a pattern here? The pattern is, yes, you. The book that you write is from your mind and it is a very personal extension of you.

By writing a book, you are sharing your ideas, knowledge and information with others. In most cases, these will be total strangers that you have never and will most likely never meet in your lifetime, but they will know you. Writing a book is a very personal journey that forces you to open your mind and your heart to your readers, in the hopes that they will gain something valuable from your work.

When it is finally published and the journey is over, you will bask in the glory of your accomplishment. The product that you created will have the potential to reach out and help others and, as a writer, this is the greatest way to extend yourself to your readers.

Reason 88

Your Book Will Bring Fun And

Endless Enjoyment

If the purpose of life as the Dalai Lama says is happiness, then writing your book will be a very integral part of the happiness you create in your life. Writing a book can be fun, but the greatest enjoyment will come from seeing your work in print and watching the joy that others receive from reading it. There's nothing like opening your e-mail and getting a message from readers who are taking the time to let you know how your book has helped them in some way.

The fun part of having a book published is being able to talk about your work and be proud of what you do. Let's face it. It's fun to talk about something that we like. If you are an author, you obviously like some aspect of the writing process. It's enjoyable to meet others who share your interest and to always know that you have written a book. Once you publish a book, you are an author and you always will be.

Reason 89

A Book Gives You Something Great To Anticipate

When you write a book, there is a lot of anticipation in how it will turn out. What will the cover look like? How will it feel to hold your book in your hands? What will it be like to see your name in newspapers and magazines as a newly published author? These are all exciting times for an author and you will soon come to know these experiences firsthand.

Beyond the actual publishing process, you will anticipate the opportunities that may arise as a result of your book. What type of career choices will become available? Who will you meet? What does the future hold? Will you be able to live anywhere you want without having to punch the time clock every day at work?

We all enjoy having something to look forward to and, if you are like most, anticipating the future with promise is a wonderful experience. Anticipation, alone, is something to look forward to. Don't you think?

Reason 90

Writing A Book Helps You With Change

So many people live their lives trying to avoid change. What most people don't realize is that the only thing that really is constant in life is change. How many times have you heard someone say something like this? As soon as I get this over with I can get back to things being normal around here again and I can relax.

These people are actually saying I won't enjoy myself until things are back to normal. People like this might as well say as soon as I get my life over with I can start to enjoy myself. Life is change and to enjoy life you must accept and embrace change. When you write a book you are making positive change in your life and the lives of your readers. You are launching a change order into the universe that will improve so many lives for the better.

Many people have a problem with change. It's easy to fall into a routine and get comfortable in what some may call a rut, but the idea behind writing a book is that you want to change something about your life. Whether it's financial, social or business, you are searching for something and your new book may just be the answer you have been looking for.

When you write a book, many things in your life will change. These changes will start out small and gradually work their way up to bigger and better occurrences. Your first new experience as an author will be the thrill of finishing your book. Then, you will be elated at your first glimpse of the finished product. As you progress through the process, you will accept the fact that people are now looking at you differently.

When all is said and done, writing a book can change your life significantly. Not so much the process of writing the book itself, but the opportunities that it can provide.

Reason 91

Raises Your Status

We are all created equal, but we definitely rise to different levels of status from our contemporaries. Although it may not be right it is a fact that many people and business associates will judge you by what you do and the status level you are currently enjoying. Your status refers to your social or professional standing, or your classification. When you write a book, your status immediately raises to a level that few other individuals will ever achieve.

Let's forget about your business status for a moment and just think about how becoming an author will affect you socially. You may begin to see the difference in the way people act around you, but the greatest change will likely be in the events that you are suddenly invited to attend. You will be networking with a new crowd, which means you will meet new people and experience new things. The keyword here is 'new' and that's just one important part of a change in your social status.

When it comes to business, you will gain the respect of colleagues and you will be able to achieve more through your career. Whether you choose to pursue consulting, public speaking or prefer to travel the world hosting seminars and appearing on national television broadcasts, you will be highly regarded as an expert after having penned your own book.

Reason 92

Attracts Better Opportunities

Just because you write a book doesn't always mean that you have to live your life as a writer. It can be the book that brings you wealth but more often than not it will be all of the opportunities that you attract from the book that will really propel your life into greater success.

When you become an author, you will gain opportunities to speak in public, host your own seminars, write other books, become a professional consultant or basically any other avenue that you choose. Once you self-publish, you are showing the world that you are capable of anything.

You can create many information products, oversee their creation, promote and market their presence and enjoy the successful benefits that follow. Can you tell me one career that these traits are not a valuable part of? Exactly. Your venture as an author will just be the first page in a very exciting book of opportunities.

Reason 93

Saves You Money

Writing a book is the best kept secret to attracting customers the marketing world has ever used. Rather than pay to advertise and acquire a new customer, you actually make money by selling a book and acquiring a customer. You in fact turn the whole customer acquisition cost upside down by writing a book.

When you write a book, you can say everything that you

need to say and do it in a way that will be available for the
world to see. If you own a business, you already know the
cost of advertising through brochure printing or booklets.
Why continue spending money on pamphlets to promote your
business when you can write a book that earns you credibility
and saves you a bundle in company brochures? After all, why
would you need a brochure when you have a book?

And best of all, your book is a product and it can be sold.
This means you can actually earn money from the very product
that is saving you money. With each book that you sell, you are
earning money. As readers get to know your business, you are
gaining their trust, but not through a paid advertisement or a
brochure. You are gaining their trust through a book, which is a
valuable resource that people will turn to time and time again.

Reason 94

Builds Equity

You write the book once, but you keep getting paid every time
your sell another copy. The time for money equation is totally
eliminated from your business plan. The book you have written
will continue to make you money and that is pure equity you
have by you writing your book. You are now the owner, not the
loaner.

Equity is the value of property and, as an author; you own
the equity in all of your work. This increases your net worth by
way of royalties, future sales, potential customers and increased
business opportunities.

The more you write, the more you grow as a writer. As this
happens, you earn the potential for more customers, increased
revenue and job offers that may have otherwise gone to someone
else. When it comes to business, the most important equity

that you can build is that within yourself and your books and information products.

Reason 95

Makes People Listen To You

I don't know why, but when something is put into print people take it much more seriously. The task of writing has the impact of getting people to read or hear your message and take it many times as gospel. It could be far from it but most people take what is written as fact and you can use this to your advantage to help your readers.

Who do you look to when you have a question? Would you prefer to get answers from an expert or a stranger on the street? If you are like most, you only want the advice from someone who you know is trustworthy, knowledgeable and experienced in your topic of concern. When you become an author, you will be that someone for a lot of people, and they will look to your for answers.

As an author, people will listen to you. Not only that, but they will really hear what you have to say. When you are considered to be an expert, everything that you say will be absorbed by your faithful readers, fans and possibly even your competitors.

Reason 96

Gives You A Very Competitive Edge

When it comes to many types of businesses, competition is can be high. Whenever there is a promotion to be had, there are plenty of names being thrown into the proverbial hat. If you want to gain a significant edge over your competition, write a book.

Aside from colleague competition, being the author of a book will give you a competitive edge over fellow authors, public speakers and consultants. Have your competitors written books? Doubtful. If they have, did they manage to get their titles distributed around the world? In this book, I will show you how to do just that. And this, my friend, will be one of the greatest secrets to your success.

Reason 97

Can Be Left In A Will

Do you know that people like Elvis Presley and James Dean have actually made more money since they have been dead than when they were alive? I think that is really incredible and you can do that for your family as well because your books and information are assets to you and can be left in your will.

Because your book is an asset and you own the rights to it, you can will an unpublished manuscript and/or future royalty payments on a published title to anyone of your choosing. In this respect, the legalities may become complicated. If you are planning to update your will to include a recently published or unpublished manuscript, consult with an estate planning attorney who has experience in publishing.

Your book and information can make many of your future generations' money if you take the time to set things up properly and legally. Don't miss out on this great opportunity of working once and being paid over and over again.

Reason 98

Best Leverage For Advertising

An ad in a newspaper is often a one time shot. Writing your book sells for you over and over again, each time someone buys and reads your book. That is really what leverage is all about-- how to get the most out of your money and your labor.

If you want to get the most out of advertising, you will use your book to get all of the media attention possible. A press release and your book can pay much bigger dividends than ads and many times the press release will be free.

Make it a point to appear on television, participate in radio interviews, and donate several copies of your book to be given away to call-in radio contestants, notify the press about upcoming book signings and send press kits and sample copies of your book to every editor who has the power to get your name into print.

If you want to influence the media to promote you and your work, don't be shy. Tell them who you are, why you wrote a book and why it is an important topic worthy of attention.

Reason 99

Get Special Treatment

Who doesn't like special treatment? Fortunes have been made giving people special treatment. My wife and I go to the same restaurant almost every week because they all know our name and give us special treatment. People love it and so will you.

When you think about individuals who you typically associate with receiving special treatment, who are they? Famous people, perhaps? As an author, you will have achieved a certain level of fame in your own right and this typically comes with some type of special treatment.

As an author, you may find that people are generally nicer to you. When you are respected, it shows. You may be given free product samples, be invited to attend certain events, or possibly even be invited to consult on important issues.

In a nutshell, the special treatment that you get largely depends on the type of work that you do, the topic of your book and the level of marketing and promotion that you achieve. The more people that know about you and your work as an author, the more likely you are to see the benefits in a variety of ways.

Reason 100

Focuses Your Talents

When you really think about it, the writing of your book automatically puts you in focus because you must tell your story or give your information in approximately 200 pages. That takes focus!

Have you ever met someone who seems to have no direction or seems to be all over the place in terms of their life? By that, I mean they either have no clue what they want out of life or they are trying so many different things that they are unable to focus on just one. Both scenarios are troubling, especially if you are the undecided subject.

Writing a book allows you to focus your talents in one particular area. More than that, it forces you to focus. It's impossible to write a book without the right amount of dedication and direction. Some people think that you have to be an expert on a topic just to write about it, but that's not the case. Yes, an expert can create a book. But a book can also create an expert.

You do not have to be a talented singer just to write about how to become one, do you? Would you have to be a movie star just to write about one? Of course not. Writing is about the combination of information and knowledge through unspoken words.

Reason 101

Caters To Your Vanity

Anyone who has written a book usually takes great pride in their work. Pride is a form of vanity and although this is not a term that most consider themselves to be, we all have a bit of vanity. The trick is to not allow it to overtake our feeling of being humble. If you need to feel good about yourself or just prefer to add another accomplishment to the list, writing a book will cater to your desire to feel good.

When you walk down the street, you cannot help but hold your head high when someone stops to talk about your latest book. Maybe you're at the grocery store, the post office or even at a restaurant when someone takes the time to stop and compliment you. What better feeling is there than for a stranger to know you? When this happens, you will know that you have attained fame. Just don't let it go to your head.

Reason 102
You Will Get Traffic From Search Engines

If you have a website, then you already know how valuable internet traffic and search engine optimization can be. But even if you don't, your book will appear online with major booksellers and they typically generate a lot of website traffic.

The content of your book can be a large source of search engine traffic if it is set this up properly on your website. As the search engines evolve and get better at bringing searchers the best and most relevant information, they will help you to grow your book business.

If you do have a website and you promote your book properly online, which we will discuss later in this book, you will be able to take advantage of one of the most valuable, and free, resources that the internet has to offer. Search engines are a powerful tool that users look to when searching for a specific keyword or phrase.

You will gain even more website traffic if you distribute a press release, which will also be discussed in detail later, through the proper networks.

When all is said and done, you could find that thousands of websites are either mentioning or linking to your own website and, in short, this means potential customers. In no time, you could find yourself on the road to riches thanks to your new website traffic.

Reason 103

Cost Effective When It Comes To Promoting & Advertising

If you are like many first-time authors, you don't have a bulging bank account. And that's okay. When it comes to the promotion and marketing aspect of your book, you will just need to get a little creative in your approach to publicity.

When you become an author, the media may very well be your best friend. By sending a simple press kit, which I will discuss later in this book, you can gain media attention that would otherwise cost you a small fortune. If you're wealthy to begin with and prefer paid advertising, that's fine, but why not also enjoy the benefits of free publicity? After all, you can't save it if you spend it. If you are on a budget, you will need to stretch your dollar for all it's worth.

You can gain print, television and radio interviews with nothing more than a little public relations footwork. And of course, once you get your book into circulation, it becomes an effective promotional and marketing tool all on its own.

Reason 104

You Will Be The Center Of Attention At Parties

How would you feel if all eyes were on you? You are the focus of a gathering, the center of attention at a party. Just imagine the personal fulfillment that you will enjoy as people dote over you.

When you are an author, you are also very popular. Everyone wants to know you, be around you and find out what you're all about. Everybody likes attention and when you become an author, you should be prepared for a lot of it.

When you walk into a room, people will notice you. You could be wearing the least impressive outfit in the room, but you will still stand out. When you write a book and become famous, which people consider authors to be, you can enjoy socializing in a whole new light.

Reason 105

Your Salesman (Book) Never Sleeps Or Takes The Day Off

In your current job, can you earn money when you shop, take a vacation or even sleep? Probably not and, if you do, then why are you reading this book? You should be writing one of your own. If you're like most people, you earn money when you're "on the clock." Not before and certainly not after.

Now, if you're an author, your job is to write and promote your book and you can earn money anytime. Morning, afternoon, evening, night, etc. You name it! Not only that, but you are receiving 24/7 of publicity with your book being in the spotlight. Books that are listed with online bookstores are always available to order and, even better, they are offered around the world. Weekdays, weekends, holidays, etc. You can earn money, customers and new business leads every day, all day and it's all thanks to one of the greatest marketing tools in existence--your book.

Reason 106

Creates A Very Lucrative
Speaking Career

If you want to jumpstart your career in public speaking, there's no better way to do it than by becoming an expert in your field of choice. At the risk of sounding like a broken record, I really feel that this bears repeating. As I've discussed so many times already, you will be considered an expert just by becoming an author.

If you want to host a seminar, you will need some type of credentials that will make people want to see and hear you. Give them a reason to want to attend your event and then give them another reason to come back again. If you already have a published book, then you must be an expert and that's who people want to listen to. After all, there's no reason to listen if something worthy isn't being said. As an expert, anything that you say demands attention.

Reason 107
There Is No Job To Retire From

This is one of the main reasons I have chosen the path I have for the rest of my life. Being an author and selling my information is my passion and to me it's like I am not working. So I ask you, if I am not working what is there to retire from?

Go For It! Don't Wait Another Day For IT To Happen!

You can be the author, expert etc. from anywhere in the world and at any age. It is a great way to add value to the world and help others go further in their life.

If there is one most important point you get from this book it is this. There is no board that will call you up and tell you that you are the expert. Don't wait another day for that to happen. You must appoint yourself the expert and gain all the extra life benefits you get from that vantage point in life.

And the best way to certify yourself as the expert is to:

"WRITE AND PUBLISH YOUR OWN BOOK"

Writing A Book May Not Make You Rich, But What The Book Can Do Will

Ok, so now that you're ready to write your book that everyone will want to read, it's time that you know the truth. Even if your book becomes a bestseller, you aren't likely to get rich from it. Why? Because the wealth that you gain from your book will likely be from the opportunities that your book creates rather than the royalties themselves.

Yes, royalties are good and they can come in handy. Who doesn't like to get paid, right? But when you look at the big picture, you will see that achieving wealth through increased product sales, business growth, and more publicity for your services and even a new career path, you will see that the real potential for income is in the benefits that your book produces.

How will your book give you everything that you want? By adding credibility to your name, giving the media a reason to write or talk about you and by attracting customers to your product or service.

What I'm trying to say is that you absolutely must write a book, but don't do it for the sole purpose of becoming wealthy from royalties. You are much more likely to become wealthy through successfully marketing your book, your business and your product or service, than by sitting back and simply collecting a royalty check every quarter.

The book that you write is not the end of your journey, but rather the beginning. If you simply sell your book and never allow it to reach it's full marketing potential, you are doing yourself and your work a great disservice. If you want to enjoy a massive stream of income, you can't be afraid to get your feet wet.

Chapter 2

Where The Rubber Meets The Road How To Avoid The Road Blocks By Vaporizing Your Excuses And Quickly Completing Your Book

Even after reading more than 100 reasons why you must write a book, I know from years of being an entrepreneur and from the many seminars I have taken that most people will not take action on one of the most important steps they can do to move their lives powerfully forward. In fact, the sad truth is that probably less than 5% of you will have started writing your book, one year from now.

Even if it only changes the life of one in a hundred people I am still a happy man because I know what it has done for the few who will take action. Because I have such a passion for showing people how much writing a book can improve their lives I am going to help you to get past you biggest hurdle which will be your own mind disguised as excuses.

If I can help people to see the ill informed logic of their excuses then I can get more people to write their books. Writing a book is such a worthwhile life endeavor that I will do whatever I have to do to make sure you take action and complete your book.

First of all, I just have to know…what are you waiting for? You already know what becoming an author can do for your life, and the fact that you are reading this book tells me that you already have the desire to enhance your career, so just lay it on me. What's the holdup? Ok, wait. Being a writer myself, I can probably guess. All writers go through the same process, the same elation and, yes, even the same doubts.

As a part of this book, I thought it would be an asset for you to not only learn why it's important for you to publish your own title, but also how to overcome some of the delay tactics that you may be using to get out of actually writing it. Don't worry. We all have them but, if you want to be an author, you have to deal with any doubts or hesitations and move forward with your publishing plan. After all, you won't get ahead if you never put the car into drive.

Excuse # 1:

"I just don't have the time."

I hear this excuse all the time but the fact is that we all have the same 24 hours each day. People make time for what they want to do it is as simple as that. Have you ever seen a golf nut say I don't have time to play golf or a TV fanatic say I don't have time to watch my favorite TV show. It simply does not happen because we always make time for what we truly want to do.

Where we try to kid ourselves is by saying something will take more time than it actually takes. I mean if you thought your book was going to take you two years of hard work to write you probably don't have that time. But the fact of the matter is that using our BRWT Force technology, which we show you how to use later in the book, you will only need about 1 hour a day for 17 days to write your entire book. So if you could write for 30 minutes per day it will still only take you about 34 days to complete.

You have to set aside the time to write, just like you do for work. You could get up an hour earlier, go to bed an hour later or take a shorter lunch break. You do have the time needed because it does not take a lot of time to write a book, contrary to what most people will tell you.

You already know what value it will add to you and your family's life so just block out some extra time each day and your book will be finished before you know it. If you spent a half hour each day reading this book you now have that half hour to put toward writing your own book.

When you think about it, you can write several books a year if you wanted to. Don't wait just get started because the investment versus the return is second to none.

Excuse # 2:

"I'm not a writer."

This is one the most ridiculous myths ever circulated by man. Bottom line is that if you can hold a conversation, then you can write a book. Most people try to complicate the writing process by trying to sound too articulate. When writers try to sound to articulate they can't write as fast and the writing is much harder to understand.

Want me to prove to you that anyone can be a good writer. Do you have a loved one, ex girl or boyfriend that use to always write you letters of love or what they were up to at that time in their life? Remember how good those letters were and how much you looked forward to them?

Now I want you to think whether that person was an avid book reader or had taken a course in writing. Almost always the answer would be no. They were merely writing the way they talk.

Don't over think this one it will stop you in your tracks you only have to be able to hold a conversation and put that conversation on paper. You will learn with our BRWT Force technology that not only can you write, but you can write fast. In fact the faster you write the better your writing will be.

I know this sounds crazy, but it is true nonetheless. You don't have to be a "writer" to write a book. Ok, I've said it. Now you know the truth. You will be a fabulous writer if you just write the way you talk.

I bet when you talk to your friends you don't use big or hard-to- understand words. If you did, you would sound ridiculous and it is the same when you write. Most of your audience will not understand the big words but all of your audience will understand the small words.

Excuse # 3:

"I'm a procrastinator."

There are many reasons why people tend to be procrastinators. They're afraid they won't write well enough, or it's not the right time or whatever excuse they believe in their own mind for why hey keep putting off the task at hand.

The excuses are endless for delay but they are also just that—excuses. None have any more legitimacy than what you give them. They are merely a figment of your imagination.

Here is the best way to break through the procrastinator's barrier:

1. Book a time to start your writing.
2. Put all thoughts or excuses out of your mind except for your starting time.
3. Realize that your starting time will be the most important thing to do and nothing will get in your way.
4. Start.

Let no other distraction enter the process because the first time you follow these steps will lead to the second time and it gets easier each time you sit down to write your book.

Once you have broken the procrastination barrier, you will find that your book will materialize quickly before your eyes. Once it is written it is done and to be enjoyed for the rest of your life and possibly longer. Your book will take on a life of its own so don't fall victim to your own thoughts of procrastination.

Excuse #4:

"I'm not motivated."

I am an incredibly lazy person, and it has been one of my biggest blessings. Now I can hear some of you say that calling yourself lazy is not a good way to talk or think about yourself. They would be right if those people thought that being lazy was a negative rather than a positive attribute. I my case being lazy is very positive.

You see, because I am so lazy it helps me to be creative in the way I get things done. I'm lazy so I don't want to spend a lot of time and energy on something so I come up with good ways to get things done quickly and easily.

Because I am lazy I don't want to have to work to hard but at the same time I want to give value to our world. For many of us, being lazy is a problem because of our up bringing. For me laziness has helped me to focus on having a super successful career without a lot of hard work.

I focus on the end result or goal, writing this book for example, because I know of all the success and opportunities it can bring you. This is one of the easiest ways for me to accomplish what I want without a lot of work.

If you are lazy like me, then you don't need a lot of motivation you just need to focus on the end result and you will be quickly writing your book and reaping all the rewards from it. I believe the writing of your book could be the easiest route to your success and abundant life so forget the motivation just take the easy route and go for the prize.

If you are starting to struggle at all, just turn around and go with the flow. When you struggle, it is your inner navigation system telling you that you are off course. Go with the flow and create the life of your dreams through the writing of your book.

Excuse # 5:

"I think I will have writer's block."

What came first, the chicken or the egg? Writer's block is merely a syndrome that someone came up with for any writer who is inept. You would think it is some sort of disease that you get as a writer, if you are not careful.

Writer's block comes when a writer gets stuck and just can't think of something to write the book forward. I guess it's a little like being lost in the woods. You stand there frozen not

knowing what way to go. As soon as you have a map you will
easily navigate yourself back out of the woods.

It is the same with writing a book if you have a good
map you will always have something to write about. The map
that I am referring to as a writer is your book outline. With a
detailed outline as we will show you in this book you will never
be at a loss for words and you will never have that trounced up
syndrome called "writer's block."

Excuse # 6:

"I'm a perfectionist."

One of the most freeing thoughts you can ever have is that
nothing is perfect. How much time and effort have perfectionists
put into thinking about how to do something perfect, and then
never get started? You will use more energy thinking about
perfection as opposed to just doing a mediocre job and getting
it done.

I am going to tell you a really big secret here. A person
who puts out a book that is just barely mediocre will ultimately
do much better than the person who waits too long to put out
the perfect book. I know because I used to play that game and I
wasted a lot of time.

I was so concerned about getting things just right and
doing all the ground work to put out the perfect product that
I would just not get some things done. I'd think that it wasn't
good enough yet or it needed more work or research.

Then for some reason, I started to notice some people who
were doing what I wanted to do that weren't as knowledgeable
or as good at a particular subject as I was, but they were really
successful in that niche. I began to notice this more and more

until I realized the one thing they had that I didn't--they were getting things done while I was still trying to be perfect.

It is a little sad when you think about it. It will never be perfect, so you just have to get over yourself and get on with it. Even bad content will get you further along than no content at all. I recommend that you have good content, but I have to tell you, that you just don't need it to be significantly more successful than you are right now.

Most of your readers will not read past page 18 of your book. That is a fact. Most people will not finish reading your book. So think about this! Even if you write a bad book, the fact is most won't know it because they won't read it.

You will still have achieved the expert status and fame of being the author of a book, regardless of how many people finish it. You might say, "but what happens if one of the people who reads it says it's not a good book?" Who cares if they say anything to you, (which I doubt would happen anyway.) You can say, "thank you for your comments" and know that you accomplished something significant.

You are already out in front of the majority of the population because you wrote a book, so don't get hung up on perfectionism because it simply doesn't pay and the perfect book doesn't exist.

Excuse # 7:

"It takes to much research."

I have to tell you I almost feel a little guilty about this one. You hear about authors that spend months, if not years, researching for the book they want to write. It is ridiculous when you think about it. If they have to spend even months researching the book they want to write perhaps they should pick a subject they know something about.

Let me tell you how I do it. Remember, I have been blessed with being lazy. First off, I do absolutely no research before I start writing. I just start to write quickly from the detailed outline that I have put together for the book. If I come to a part in the book I need a specific date, statistic or some other fact, then I will mark that spot in the book and do the research later.

By doing it this way I only have to get the answers to specific questions that still need answered after I have written the book. I mean why would you do the research before you write the book you would just be wasting your time looking for things you are not sure you will need for the book yet? You're over researching!

If that isn't the lazy way what about this? Sometimes I will even re-word the part of the book I need to do research for. For example if I am writing about a certain battle in history and I have to find out what date it was rather than having to go to the trouble of finding the exact date I might reword that part of the story to say the battle in the early 1500's so I may not need the exact date.

I must caution you on this because you must realize that accuracy of information affects your credibility so don't be inaccurate or vague if it will affect you in a negative way. With the internet most information can be found very quickly. Unless the information offers the reader a specific benefit, it is probably not useful to place in your book, or waste the time researching.

Can you see what a blessing laziness can be? I mean isn't that why we invented the automobile, because we got too lazy to walk anywhere? So don't make a big ordeal out of writing your book, it does just not require a lot of research if you do it right.

Excuse # 8:

"I'm not talented enough."

I am not asking you to cure AIDS and cancer and be the first person to win 5 Nobel Peace Prizes. All as I am asking is that you write a book. You have the talent! Anyone who can hold a conversation has the talent to write a book. Get off the "I am not worthy" victim bandwagon and get on with it. You're worthy and don't let anyone tell you otherwise.

Any of the possible negative comments you might get about your book will be totally outweighed by the accolades you will get for completing your book. How come the ones who give all the armchair opinions aren't writing their own book? They aren't writing their own book because of all the energy they waste criticizing others. If you give lots of benefits and value to the reader they will be very delighted and happy with what they receive.

You have an obligation to share your information, in your own unique way, with others. You must be the change that people aspire to and by writing your book if you inspire others to do more and be more, then you have done a great service for all.

Even if you still don't believe you have the talent to write your book, just start with the system in this book and act as if you do. By the time you finish writing you will wonder why you ever had a doubt in your mind. The process of writing and doing the exercises will reinforce the fact that you do in fact have the talent to write your book.

Excuse # 9:

"I don't have what it takes."

If you have no formal writing training, then you most assuredly have what it takes. Let me explain. Many times in the brick and mortar industry that I was in for years, I would hire trade people who had gone out of business. I would then train them with our company. You would think with some experience in a certain trade that they would be easy to train and get started, but this was not usually the case.

It was usually easier to train someone from scratch, than it was getting someone with experience to first unlearn their old ways and then learn new ways. More often than not, the ones without experience did better with our training system.

I have had other business friends, in other sectors, which found very much the same thing and even had some friends who owned restaurants and refused to hire people that had worked at other restaurants. So what I am saying is, that the very fact you say you don't have what it takes is good indicator that you will do well, and have what it takes to write your book.

If you follow the system you read in this book without any preconceived ideas, you will do just fine and will amaze yourself.

Excuse # 10;

"I don't have a plan to follow to write a book."

Even though no previous experience is needed to write a book you do certainly need a plan to follow for a successful book. With a plan you will know what your book will look like from start to finish before you ever even start to write.

You have a plan to follow in this book that allows you to know where you are going and to stay on course. When you have a laid out plan and outline you will be able to quickly and easily write your book and not stray off course. Your plan gives you even for flexibility to be creative within your plan without getting lost or off track.

Many writers who have no plan will wander off course and end up writing many pages they realize later will not even fit anywhere in their book. This is a waste of time that you won't run into by following the plan in this book.

Not only will a plan and good outline save you a lot of time it will give you the most flowing and organized book you will be proud of.

Chapter 3

How To Get From 0 To 60 In Seven Seconds Flat!

SIMPLE STEPS TO WRITING YOUR BOOK

One of the biggest obstacles to being an author is completing or even getting started on your book.

Don't let this happen to you.

This is too important. If you have the ability to turn $5 into $500 do you sit on it and say "I'll do it tomorrow." Or do you run to the bank and get as many 5 dollar bills as you can? Hopefully you run to the bank! I'm telling you to run to the bank with your book!

You have two choices on how to get to the bank. Your first option is to write the book yourself.

The advantage to writing the book yourself is that you:

1. Retain all of the control over the content of the book.

2. Retain control over the voice of your book.

3. Retain control over the structure and tone of your book.

Writing the book yourself will save you money but cost you time. Your other option is to hire a ghostwriter. There are of course advantages and disadvantages to hiring a ghostwriter.

1. If you hire a ghostwriter you will save yourself time.

2. If you write your book, it will be 100% you. If you hire a ghostwriter, it will be partially them. That's not necessarily a bad thing, if you and your ghostwriter

are simpatico but if you're not, you may find that your identity is lost.

3. Ghostwriters cost $.

4. You lose the satisfaction of creating a book when you hire a ghostwriter.

5. You may end up with a product that you are unhappy with.

Let's first look at writing your book yourself...

How Do I Write My Book In As Little Time As Possible?

I'm sure you've heard some best selling authors say that it took them ten years to write a book.

Come on! Really? That's like 4 words a day. What were they doing the rest of the time because it certainly doesn't take 8-12 hours to write 4 words.

My guess is that:

1. They're stretching the truth—a lot!

2. They get caught in a literary quagmire of what it means to be a great writer.

3. They really didn't have a clue what they were writing about nor did they make any time in their day to do it.

Skipping the first excuse, let's look at excuse number two first.

What Does It Mean To Be A Great Writer?

Take a look at 5 of your favorite books—it doesn't matter if they are fiction or non fiction—it's just important that they are books that you consider to be good books. Books that you have enjoyed, received a benefit from, and would consider them quality books. Now, open each book and read a few paragraphs.

What you'll likely notice is that there is a common theme running in all of them.

They're written conversationally.

Think about that for a moment. Conversationally. They're written like you talk. Conversational style is the best style because it is easy to read, easy to understand and easy to write.

You can talk, right?

IF YOU CAN TALK, THEN YOU CAN WRITE.

One of the most prolific writers and arguably one of the best commercial fiction writers today is Elmore Leonard. If you haven't read him, go to the library and check out a book. You'll have hundreds of titles to choose from and any book you choose will be a great ride! I'm sure you're familiar with his work. Both movies, Get Shorty and Out of Sight were based on Elmore Leonard's books.

Why am I talking about Elmore Leonard? He writes very conversationally. He's not confused about what it means to be a great writer; he's too busy writing and selling books! And he has a fantastic conversational style, in fact his books are 80-90% dialogue and it works. He is also prolific and manages to crank out several best sellers every year. Which means that he is certainly writing more than 4 words a day.

But I'm writing non-fiction you say. Great, even easier because you don't have to worry about plot! Conversational style, or writing like you talk, could be broken down into several seemingly difficult steps but I'm going to make it easy.

Ready...?

BRWT

What?

BRWT. (PRONOUNCED BRUTE) IT STANDS FOR BRAIN RUSH WRITING TECHNIQUE. (AKA BRWT FORCE TECHNOLOGY)

This is how BRWT works. Please don't be surprised by its simplicity. Don't doubt it. Just try it and I guarantee it will work. Here's BRWT in action:

When you sit down to write, don't stop. Don't check your email; don't correct your spelling or grammar. Write as the words and ideas rush into your brain. Dump everything you have to say onto your paper as fast as your pen or typing fingers can keep up.

But it will be a huge mess, you say?

Maybe. Probably not. If you follow your book plan, definitely not. More on your book's plan in a little bit.

Here's a little secret. Write your copy like you're writing to a friend.

Letters to friends are easy to write, right? The words flow easily onto the page and you'll probably notice that you use the word "you" often. That is a key to conversational style.

Your book is about helping your reader. They want to be involved in the content. They want to feel like you're writing it just for them. I know that I do when I read a book.

Now let's pause for a moment. When you write a letter to a friend, assuming that you have several topics to discuss, you don't mix the topics up. There is an organization to your letter. You probably start with the idea that is going to be the strongest and most interesting.

You're also going to start a new paragraph with each new idea or topic.

Your book will be organized in much the same way. Note that the great thing about writing a book is that you don't have to write it in order. You can work on any section independently and then put it together in the order that makes the most sense.

How do you organize your book into topics?

Step-By-Step Approach to Creating your Book plan.

This is important if you're going to write a book. When you sit down to your desk, and prepare to use the BRWT you have to know what you're writing, right?

Here's how to do it:

My Secret 7 Step System To Write Any Book Lightening Fast

Step 1.

Decide how long you want your book to be. The average book is 200 to 300 pages, which means 20 to 30 chapters assuming that each chapter is approximately ten pages.

Step 2.

Write down 20 to 30 topics that you want to cover in your book. These will be chapters so the topics need to be broad enough to cover 10 pages. If you've decided that your book will be about 200 pages then you'll need 20 chapters/topics. Rather than sit down and write 20 topics, you need to write 25. Yes, write 5 more chapter titles than you think you'll need.

If you can only come up with twenty potential topics, then push yourself to come up with 5 more. Even if they seem off the wall or irrelevant. Also, look to the topics that have an abundance of information and can be divided into more than one chapter.

Conversely, if you find that you have 50+ ideas, great then plan for a second book. Nobody wants to read a 500 page book.

Step 3.

Take a look at the topics that you're going to address in your book. What strikes you as the most interesting, strongest, and most compelling topic? Unsure? Ask your friends, family, and associates which topic is most compelling. Once you've established what topic/chapter is the most compelling, make that chapter one.

Order the subsequent chapters in a logical progression. Keep in mind that you're ordering the chapters for your reader, not for how you'd prefer to write the book.

Step 4.

After you have established 25 chapter topics and have ordered them, eliminate the weakest 5 chapters. They may be the 5 topics that you forced yourself to create, but you might be surprised to find that your weakest topics are topics that you originally thought would be good chapters. Don't fuss. Cut them right out and forget about them. You want your book to be the strongest most compelling book possible. Be ruthless.

Step 5.

Write down ten to fifteen points that you must cover in each chapter. Like this:

Chapter One Bringing Your Dog Home

1. Dog proofing the house
2. Introducing other pets
3. Introducing small children and other family members
4. Feeding times
5. Potty Training
6. Sleeping arrangements
7. Establishing an exercise routine
8. Who's the boss?
9. Know the rules before they arrive
10. Playtime

Step 6.

Turn each point into a question that you need to answer for your friend/reader.

Like this:

- How can you dog proof your house effectively and efficiently?
- What is the first thing you do when you bring your dog home?
- Who is the top dog? Where does your dog rank in the family order?

Why change the statements into questions? Because, it is much easier to answer a question than it is to defend or explain a statement.

Step 7.

BRWT. Answer these questions as fast as you can using the brain rush writing technique. Choose the questions that are easiest to answer first to build your momentum and to get a handle on how the technique works. Don't stop to check your spelling. Don't stop to research anything. Think about it! You don't stop to research or edit your conversations so don't stop writing. The secret is to write as fast as possible in your own conversational style.

Don't pause for any reason. Pour all of the information as it comes into your head and put it on paper. This is important. Writing like this not only produces an abundance of copy, 9 times out of 10 the copy is well written and will require very little editing and revision. This is because you're writing like you talk. You're not taking the time to edit yourself or to find your literary muse; you're simply writing down what you know as you know it.

It is important that you address one question at a time and that you write for a designated amount of time. Give each question 5-7 minutes, no longer. Why? Because if you give yourself too long to answer a question, you'll have the tendency to fill the time second guessing yourself and falling away from the BRWT Force. On the other hand if you know that you only have 5 minutes to dump all of your information onto the paper, you're not going to pause, you're not going to get up to sharpen your pencil or refill your coffee cup. You're going to write and you're going to write hard. Besides, you can wait five minutes to refill your coffee.

After five minutes, move onto the next question and repeat the process.

Now I want you to take a step back and do the math.

20 chapters divided into 10 question equals 200 sections. 200 sections times five minutes a section equals 1000 minutes. If you write for an hour a day, that's only addressing twelve five minute questions per day, it will take you just over 17 days to write your book. 17 DAYS!

Of course if you want to write a 300 page book then you'll add another 10 chapters, which is 100 questions. 100 questions at 5 minutes per question is 500 minutes. At one hour a day, the additional 100 pages will take you approximately nine days.

This means that if you choose to write a 300 page book, it'll take you a total of 26 days to complete your first draft!

Don't have 60 minutes a day? Then commit to 30 minutes a day. Surely you have 30 minutes a day to devote to writing a book that is going to change your life. REALLY CHANGE YOUR LIFE! 30 minutes a day for a 200 page book means that it will only take you 34 days to finish your first draft.

On the other hand, think about what you can accomplish if you devote more than an hour per day to writing your book!

Let's talk about time….

How On Earth Do You Find An Extra Hour A Day?

This part is up to you. I cannot force you to write. You're going to have to make time each and every day to work on your book. How much time you devote is up to you. Ten minutes a day, great. The first draft of your book will be done in three months. That's certainly a reasonable amount of time and surely you have ten minutes a day, right?

The faster you complete your book, the faster you'll achieve your personal, career, and financial goals. The sooner you'll be able to say, "by the way, have you seen my new book?"

Remember your 101 reasons for writing a book?

They won't happen unless you commit yourself to writing each and every day!

To optimize your time, find a time of day that you're likely to be most productive and motivated. If you're a morning person, don't set aside 20 minutes after the 11:00 news and before you go to bed as your designated writing time. It won't happen. Likewise, if you're a night owl, don't tell yourself that you'll get up half an hour early every day to write. I've been there and it doesn't work.

Set aside time during your most productive time of day!

ESTABLISH A WRITING PLAN THAT WORKS FOR YOU

When you are first getting started on your book, it is important to find your most productive time of day. Find the time of day that you are at your creative best. If you are an early morning person, then deciding to work on your book after Lost and before you go to bed is not the best idea. It won't happen. Maybe the quiet hours before everyone wakes will be your best time. Conversely, if you're a night owl, then hoping to get up an hour earlier every day won't work and maybe writing while the late show is on will be your best time.

In addition to finding the best time for you to write, you'll need to consider the best or most optimal location for you to write. It might be your kitchen table, or the local coffee shop, or a home office. I've known writers to sequester themselves in their car during lunch to get an hour's worth of writing time.

Your plan might also include how long you are able to write. You'll not only want to consider how long your attention span can focus on your story, but writers also have a tendency to get deeply involved in their projects and neglect their other responsibilities. So keep in mind how long you can reasonably spend on your book each day without neglecting your loved ones!

Other factors that you might want to consider are the materials that you're going to need. Using the BRWT Force, will you write in a notebook or directly onto your computer? Consider also, using a voice recorder to record your thoughts and have someone transcribe them.

Quick And Easy Editing. A 5 Day Plan So You Don't Get Bogged Down In The Process!

Editing is part of the writing process and there is no way around it. That being said, I want to break the editing process down into quick and easy steps and I don't want to spend too much time on the topic.

Nothing is perfect so don't edit forever. Give yourself a week and be done with it.

Day 1. Fix all spelling and grammar with your computer's spelling and grammar check. Follow through with a quick read to make sure all of the contractions are correct. Example, you're and your, it's and its. The computer will often miss these contraction errors.

Day 2. Do a quick search of passive words like 'can' and make them active. Can becomes must or will. Also search for boring verbs and jazz them up. Runs becomes sprints, dashes, darts for example. Search for adverbs and get rid of them when possible. For example, "talks quietly" becomes "whispers."

Day 3. Cut the crap. Face it, there will be paragraphs that just don't work. Don't spend hours trying to make them work. Cut them. It's done. Move on.

Day 4. Add transitions between paragraphs where needed.

Day 5. Add strong leads and compelling hooks. You hook your reader by pulling them into your copy with attention grabbing paragraphs right at the

beginning of each chapter, called a "lead," and leave
them wanting more at the end of each chapter,
called a 'hook."
That's it. You're done editing. Not convinced? Fine, hire
an editor but don't let this process drag on for too long. You
have money to make and NOTHING IS PERFECT! Remember
that a finished mediocre book will always outperform a never
completed perfect book. There is no such thing as a perfect
book.

So now you might be thinking, never mind, I don't want to
write it myself. Let's address the topic of hiring a ghostwriter.

DEFINING A GHOSTWRITER

We've all heard the title, but what exactly is a ghostwriter? As
the name implies, a ghostwriter is a writer that contributes to
a project, but is not seen or heard by the reader. Similar to a
behind-the-scenes individual, a ghostwriter is instrumental in
the development of a writing project.

If you are writing a book, for instance, you may run into
a few snags along the way. This is where a ghostwriter would
come in by offering their writing expertise and granting
you permission to use the work in any way that you choose.
In exchange for giving you the copyrights to the work, the
ghostwriter would be paid at a predetermined fee.

Ghostwriters do not receive credit for their work in the way
that a typical writer does. Where a writer normally receives a
byline, a ghostwriter does not. In a typical agreement between
you and a ghostwriter, you would be granted the exclusive
copyrights to the work. This means that you can put your name
on it and publish it as a book, resell it to someone else or edit
the work as you choose. In fact, a lot of people do this. When
you own the copyrights to the work, you can do with it as you
please.

If you choose to hire a ghostwriter, be clear on what rights
you are purchasing. In most cases, the fee will vary depending

on what type of rights you require. Exclusive rights, for instance, will be more expensive. But, they also give you the freedom and flexibility to do as you please with the work itself.

A ghostwriter could be anyone. They could be an experienced journalist, published author, college student or simply someone who has the desire to start writing and wishes to dip their toe into the industry as a silent contributor at first.

How to Know if You Need A Ghostwriter

If you are working on a book or just thinking about starting a new project, you may need to seek the assistance of a professional ghostwriter. It is our recommendation that you write your book yourself because it is easy if you follow our system in this book. But if you still resist doing the job yourself it is still better to have your book out there even if it is written by a ghostwriter than to not have a book at all.

The first and most obvious sign that you need a ghostwriter is when you realize that your book is just not getting started even though you are very enthusiastic about getting your book out there. Perhaps you are at a total loss for getting started or you just need a little assistance in getting your word and page count up to a place where it should be. Of course, hiring a ghostwriter to help build on your existing outline may lead to a fresh voice that could reveal additional topics that you could use to make your book even better.

Did you know that some people who publish books aren't writers at all? That's right. They simply hire a ghostwriter to do the work, pay them for their contribution and then publish the book under their own name, while reaping the benefits. The same is true with web content, published articles and even professionally recorded songs. People hire ghostwriters for an assortment of different reasons.

Another indication that you may need to hire a ghostwriter is that you have just not blocked out the time you need to devote to writing. Whether you have a full-time job, family obligations or other chores that are keeping you from completing your book within a timely manner, a ghostwriter can do the work for you. As the copyright owner, you have full control over the content that is written. You will have the opportunity to provide the ghostwriter with an outline and will have the final approval on all work that is done. Just because you hire someone to write for you doesn't mean that you are losing creative control over the project.

Still not sure if you may need a ghostwriter? Well, I can tell you that if you are reading this section and still searching for the answer to this question, you could probably use some assistance. The mere fact that you are thinking about hiring a ghostwriter indicates that you probably need one, so take a look around, accept bids, and look over the resumes of several writers who you feel can deliver the content that you are looking for. Later in this section, I will show you where to find a professional writer to help ease some of the literary stress that you may be experiencing.

The Benefits of Hiring a Ghostwriter

Ok, so now that we know what a ghostwriter is, we need to learn the benefits of hiring one. Below are five benefits that you can experience if you choose to outsource your book to a professional writer:

1. **Professional writing.** When you hire a professional, you would obviously expect the highest quality work possible. If you choose wisely and carefully select your writer from eligible candidates, then you are sure to get the type of writing that you desire.

   If the ghostwriter you hire is a professional, he/she will accept feedback and work closely with you throughout the project to ensure that every stage is completed to your satisfaction.

2. **Saves you time.** When you hire a ghostwriter, you are saving yourself a lot of time writing. This leaves you more time to plan for the promotion of your book, design the cover, work with distributors or just continue working in your daily operations without the added stress of having to work against a book deadline.

Time is money, but it's also a precious commodity. You can use your spare time to do whatever you choose, including spend time with family, relax or just plan for the future. When your book is ready, you will be proofreading it and checking for any needed corrections. Don't put your feet up quite yet because there's still work to do but, with the help of a ghostwriter, your load will be lighter.

3. **Work directly with a writer and eliminate unnecessary overhead.** If you have ever thought about hiring someone from a writing firm or other professional organization, don't. Why pay the extra money that you will be spending simply to pay the firm for their administrative service. In addition to earning enough to show a profit, the company will also have to charge a fee that will allow them to pay their employees. This adds up quickly and, when you are on a budget, the cost can even be prohibitive.

If you work directly with a freelancer using some of the resources that I will be outlining later in this section, you will be eliminating a large portion of the overhead. In fact, the only costs you will be paying is the fee that your ghostwriter charges for the project. Most freelancers prefer to work independently, which means you will have a large selection of professionals to choose from if you know where to look.

4. **Provides a fresh voice.** When you write a book, the input you may get from another person such as a ghostwriter may give you some new ideas. A

ghostwriter is a unique individual who has his or her own ideas and talents, which could mean big things for your project. The professional that you choose could give you an entirely new view on the subject and may give you the boost that you need to get your book the attention that it deserves.

5. **Original content.** When you hire a ghostwriter and purchase exclusive rights to the work, you know that you are getting original content that has not been used elsewhere in the past and, by virtue of the contract you would put in place with the author, will not be used again in the future. Original content is, you guessed it, original.

WHAT TO LOOK FOR WHEN HIRING A GHOSTWRITER

Hiring a ghostwriter to help write your book is much like filling any other position. Before making your choice, you will need to look at a number of factors that can help to make your decision a little more clear.

First and foremost, what type of book are you hoping to have written? This is important because you will want to find a writer who has experience with similar projects. Not only that, but having previously written in a professional capacity will also be a big plus.

The next quality to look for in a ghostwriter is affordability. Their fees should be reasonable for the task being performed, but should also be within your budget. Once you begin accepting bids on your book project, you will see that ghostwriters are located all across the globe and, as such, their fees vary. As a buyer, you may not want to pay for the entire project upfront. A nice compromise is paying some type of a deposit up front and periodic payments throughout the project. In most cases, writers will request a deposit of up to one half of the total project price and the remaining balance due at the conclusion.

Another important quality in a ghostwriter is his/her ability to get the work completed in a timely manner. You probably already have a preset time that you would like to have the book completed, so look for someone who can get the job done on time.

What is the single most important career trait of a writer? You guessed it. Writing! As such, your potential ghostwriter should have samples of his/her writing that you can review. This will give you a good indication as to his/her style, grammar and ability to convey a message in a clear and concise manner. This doesn't mean that he or she must produce samples from a previously published book, but perhaps an article or report would give you a sufficient look at their writing ability.

Once you are sure that you have the right person for the job, take one more moment to think about the communication and whether or not it has flowed with ease. When you are working on a book with someone, you will need to communicate with them often. This means that the writer should be personable, willing to accept feedback, and able to respond to your correspondence within 24 hours. Even if everything looks good on paper, your personality needs to click with that of your freelancer. Otherwise, you may just end up in a bind with your new book project.

WORKING WITH A GHOSTWRITER

Choosing to hire a ghostwriter for your project could work well if you decide to go this route. As is the case with any business agreement, certain guidelines should be followed to make sure that the arrangement is a mutually beneficial and pleasant experience.

Working with a ghostwriter should be an easy task providing you get all of the details confirmed before the project begins. For instance, how much will the writer be paid, when will the project be completed and what payment terms are expected? It is not at all uncommon for a writer to request a 33% to 50% deposit up front with the remaining balance due upon completion of the project. In fact, most professional writers will require this before accepting any new assignment. Why? Quite simply, it ensures that the buyer (that's you!) is serious about the project and intends to follow through with the payments as agreed.

As the buyer, it will be up to you to let the writer know what you want. If you have a book outline already in place which you really should, provide it for reference. If you have an idea or angle instead of an actual outline, that's okay too but I must caution you that if you have an outline for your ghostwriter you will probably end up with a much better book.

Just be sure that your writer understands the message that you are trying to convey in the book and what you expect as far as page and word count. Many writers do not handle graphics, so be ready to take care of the artwork yourself or hire a graphic designer for that aspect of your book.

Before an assignment begins, always clear up any questions surrounding copyright issues and whether or not you are purchasing exclusive rights to the work. Most buyers prefer to purchase only original content and the majority also request exclusive rights to sell, distribute, edit or otherwise transfer the work in any way that they see fit.

Speaking of agreements, some assignments are done with contracts and others are completed in good faith. If you have a written record and agreement in any form, including e-mail, you can always save this for easy retrieval and reference of the agreement.

CHECKLIST FOR HIRING A FREELANCE GHOSTWRITER

- Decide on a book topic and create a detailed outline or

angle. This will help your writers to get the exact idea of the work that you need and how to best complete it. Having an accurate mental picture of your book will save time for both you and your freelancer.

- Review resumes, writing samples and past work experience for potential ghostwriters. This will give you a detailed look at the writer's experience. After all, you wouldn't hire an employee without first knowing whether or not they are qualified to do the job. When hiring a writer, the process is no different. Choosing a professional that can get the job done and done well will be your first concern.

- Narrow your selection down to only those who you feel are qualified. Once you begin accepting bids on your project, you will need to narrow the field down to those who can produce the type of work that you are looking for. Writers will bid on your job in much the same way a general contractor places a bid on a construction project. Later in this book, you will learn where to find professional freelancers who will compete for your project. Now all you will need to do is to choose the right man/woman for the job.

- Compare the response times on your communication with each potential writer. When you hire a writer, you will appreciate prompt communication. For this reason, you should take a close look at the response times for each of your candidates. If they aren't quick to respond now during the competition phase, you have to wonder how quickly they will reply after being hired. You will appreciate consistency and not just someone who wants the work, but isn't willing to earn it.

- Discuss payment terms, completion time and exclusivity for the work. These are very important issues that must be clarified in advance. You will need to know how much the writer will charge for completing the project, how and when they wish to be paid, their approximate completion date and what type of rights they are granting for the project.

- Make sure that your writer understands the direction you want to take with your book. This will save any misunderstandings and/or delays throughout the project. Be clear with your instructions and confirm that the writer is prepared and capable of completing the job accurately. This doesn't mean that there won't be questions along the way, but there must be a general feeling that the two of you are on the same page when it comes to developing your book.

- Finalize any agreements regarding payment, completion dates and revisions. Once you are certain of the writer you wish to hire, finalize any unresolved concerns regarding the aforementioned issues. Trust me when I tell you that you do not want to have anything popping up in the midst of the project that could cause friction or delays.

- Choose the writer that best suits your project and style. Congratulations! You're now ready to choose a writer and you know what you want. Make sure that the tone and style of the writer's work is what you are looking for. Most people write the way that they speak, which means you cannot expect a freelancer to change their style. It is what it is and, once you review samples, you will be able to easily choose the right professional for your project. Once you have found the best candidate, accept their proposal and get started.

WHERE TO FIND FREELANCERS

Elance (5 of 5 stars)

Rating: Competitive freelancers; Constantly updated with new job postings
http://www.elance.com
A subscription-based freelance bidding website that connects freelance programmers, web & logo designers, copywriters, illustrators and consultants with buyers.

Scriptlance (3 of 5 stars)

Rating: Regular job postings
http://www.scriptlance.com
A freelance bidding website, which requires no subscription, that connects freelance web designers, illustrators, writers and software programmers with buyers.

WriterLance (3 of 5 stars)

Rating: Occasional job postings
http://www.writerlance.com
A freelance bidding website, which requires no subscription, that connects freelance web designers, illustrators, writers and software programmers with buyers.

Freelance (unrated)

Rating: None; No experience dealing with this website
http://www.iFreelance.com
A subscription-based freelance bidding website that connects freelance programmers, web & logo designers, copywriters, illustrators and consultants and buyers.

COMBINING THE BEST OF BOTH WORLDS: HOW SOME OF THE BEST SELLING BOOKS HAVE BEEN WRITTEN BY GETTING OTHERS TO WRITE IT FOR YOU.

Have you ever heard of Chicken Soup for The Soul? Of course

you have. Chances are you've even read one of the many books published. Jack Canfield and Mark Victor Hansen have made billions of dollars off of his single idea of having other people write inspirational, motivational stories and combining them into one super marketable package. FYI, Chicken Soup For the Soul was originally self-published!

The Secret by Rhonda Byrne is another book that was put together by a team of contributors, including Jack Canfield.

So now you have decided how the book is going to be written, but what on earth are you going to write about?

How To Choose A Money Making, Career Building, Best Selling Book Topic.

The topic that you choose to write on is critical. It is safe to say that not every topic is worthy of a 200 page book. How to Choose the Best Sunscreen for example, wouldn't be a great topic. Not because there isn't a need for that information but because there isn't enough information to fill a book.

That being said, the volume of information or content, isn't your first priority when deciding what to write about. What do you think is the most important aspect when deciding your book's topic?

Demand.

Demand for your information is the most important factor when beginning to write a book. If you're pursuing a fiction career, look no farther than the bookstore shelves or the Bestseller's lists on Amazon and in your local paper to find out what is in demand.

You'll likely find two things: Commercial fiction is driven by women. Women account for more than 60% of the fiction market and 80% of the books bought by women are in the romance genre.

Don't want to write a romance? Mystery and suspense are

still big sellers and the Science Fiction and Paranormal genres are growing again in popularity.

Developing Your Story, a Fiction Writer's Path to a Perfect Plot

If you're a fiction writer and a story has yet to surface in your imagination, then there are a couple of methods to find inspiration.

Brainstorm. Sit down at your desk with an open mind, a pen, and a notebook and brainstorm a list of potential storylines. Don't edit yourself, don't judge the storyline or its potential. Let your creativity soar with this project.

Once you have a list of potential storylines to choose from, outline your favorites. You don't need to solve every problem and answer every question. Simply try to develop a beginning, middle, and end to each possibility. If you want to take it a step further, then use the tools presented in this book to develop your book's plan. Break your fiction book into 20-30 chapters (don't forget to add 5 possible chapters)

Order them as they would occur in your book, placing the most interesting chapter first!

Break each chapter up into ten scenes or events, turn those scenes into questions. For example:

Scene from Wizard of Oz: Dorothy opens the door to her home to find a world of Technicolor wonder.

Question: What does Dorothy see when she opens her front door?

Now, when you begin to write the scene, you can describe it in all of its glory, as if you were explaining it to a friend!

Back to brainstorming, I've used this brainstorming method on a number of occasions. I usually end up with 10 to 20 pages of copy for each storyline. I choose the best one and store the others in a file. I must admit that when I'm having a difficult writing day, I often return to these old pages for comfort. It's like looking at an old family photo album or reading an old diary.

Write what you like to read. Writing what you like to read is a great way to begin your own book because you already have a strong knowledge about the requirements of the genre.

If you read suspense novels, you know that the copy has to be action packed. Your hero or heroine has to constantly overcome obstacles and these obstacles need to further your plot. Likewise, if you write romance, you know that the relationship is the strongest plot line and the conflict has to relate to the two people trying to connect.

Find inspiration in the world. Newspapers, magazines, television programs, conversations with friends and family, and the evening news are full of crazy stories and inspiration. I have many friends that are in the customer service business and many of them tell interesting stories about the people they meet which could be made into a great book.

Borrow a Plot, or buy one for .99

Take a look at the most famous, popular, or even your favorite plots. Find one that has sold millions, a real bestseller, and borrow it.

I'm not talking about copyright infringement. I'm simply telling you that plots are borrowed, and modified, all the time. Romeo and Juliet is a plot that has been borrowed millions of times. West Side Story is classic Romeo and Juliet. Boy meets girl, family and friends try to keep the two apart, it ends in tragedy and death.

Find a winning plot, and make the plot your own. Change the characters, change the setting, and change the situation that causes the conflict. Change as much as you can but keep the central plot.

Choosing Your Non-Fiction Topic, Your Two Step Process

With non-fiction there are two steps. You first need to choose your potential subject matter and then you need to make sure that there is enough demand for your subject to warrant a book. It is perfectly fine, and perhaps even advisable to choose several topics in the beginning. For example, if you are an expert on raising Poodles then you could write about:

- Raising poodles,
- Breeding poodles,
- Training poodles,
- Training dogs,
- Breeding dogs,
- How to find the best breed for your family and so on.

Let's begin with the first step, choosing your subject matter.

Step #1 Choosing Your Subject

Write what you know. This, I believe, is the strongest determiner for a topic and for the potential success of your book. Writing is about sharing knowledge and passions. If you're an expert on something, then you should share it with the world.

For example, if you're an expert on dog training, then you should write a book about dog training. If you're well-versed on the subject of hydroponics and alternative gardening, then your knowledge would be well suited for a "How-To" book on the same subject.

If you are an expert at matchmaking or goal setting, then you likely have enough resources for a book and potentially some very interesting personal anecdotes on the subject matter.

Being an expert on a subject doesn't mean that you know all there is to know about the topic. You should still consult with other experts to not only have a fresh perspective, but to make sure that you're covering your topic as completely as you can to make the book as valuable to your readers as it can possibly be.

Write about what interests you. Now this isn't to say that if you are an expert in basketball but you have an interest in learning to rock climb that you shouldn't write about learning to climb. You could incorporate your learning process into a book for others that are interested in learning to rock climb. So writing what you know doesn't necessarily mean that you have to write what you know right now. You can write about a topic that interests you.

Write what is in demand. While it seems like fiction is where the money is (just look at the displays near the checkout lines at the grocery or drug store), according to statistics provided by BookWire and the American Association of Publishers, non-fiction writing accounts for 93% of all published material and the majority of the money that is made in publishing.

Why so high?

We read to learn, we read to share information, and we read to get better at something and to improve our status in life. In fact, the internet and our ability to instantly access information has meant an increase in the number of non-fiction books sold.

We are a society that demands constant improvement. We expect, to be able to grow and improve our lives and our station and we often approach this betterment by buying books!

In fact, there are really only a handful of reasons that people buy non-fiction books.

1. To make money. (If you go to the bookstore, I bet you can find more than 100 books with the word Millionaire in them! In fact, just think about how popular the "Rich Dad, Poor Dad" books are.)

2. To save energy or effort. (Quick and Easy Ways to…fill in the blank. Lose weight, Get Married, Get Divorced…)

3. To save time. (Sell Your Home in 10 days, 30 Minute Meals...)

4. To be healthier. (10 Ways to Eat Organically, How to Eliminate Fatigue, How to Manage Stress...)

5. To be popular, prettier, sexier, smarter, or better at something. (How to Meet Women, How to Be Successful, 10 Days to Better Skin, 10 Days to a Better Sex Life, etc...)

6. Spiritual guidance. (Just look at the recent success of The Secret and its many spin offs!)

Step #2 Researching Demand

This is important! If you don't have a market for your book, you're wasting your time writing it. Once you've established a topic or subject matter that you'd like to write about, you need to determine if there is a market for it.

Ask your friends, family, and associates. Establish a list of potential topics that you can write about. Try to come up with at least 5 but no more than 10. Email this list to your friends, family, associates, and even your customers, and ask them which topic they would most likely want to read about. Don't ask them which topic is their favorite or which one sounds the best. Ask them which topic they would most like to read about. This is important. You want them to make the decision based on their needs. If you ask 100 people and more than half choose the same topic, even if a third of them choose the same topic, you have a winner.

Seek out experts. One of the best ways to determine the marketability of your topics is to speak with people in the same field.

For example, if you're writing about how to work with a recruiter, then you might ask recruiters and human resource professionals for their thoughts on not only the main topic of the book but also for content ideas. You might also consider interviewing them. These interviews can very likely trigger an idea that could inspire you or be the next best seller.

Utilize the Internet. You can find information about your market and their needs by visiting online chat rooms, forums, newsgroups, blogs, and survey sites. A forum on gardening might give you a dozen ideas about problems that gardeners need help solving and then you have your book topics! You can also participate in the forums and ask people what their biggest problem is.

Keyword research. Another method for researching your topic is to search online for the keywords associated with your topic. This will not only tell you how much information is already available on your topic, but it can also give you an idea of the demand for information.

This will be helpful in determining the marketability of your book, particularly if you're writing a book, as well as a useful tool when it comes time for you to market your book.

There are many keyword tools available on the Internet. One of the most common is the Google keyword popularity tool, https://adwords.google.com/select/KeywordToolExternal. It works as follows. You first enter words that you feel people might use to find your book.

For example, if your book is going to be on Diabetes, then relevant keywords and keyword phrases might be "Preventing Diabetes," "Living With Diabetes," "Outsmarting Diabetes," etc...

Enter these keywords into the search tool and Google will show you the general volume of people that have looked for that type of information using those very same keywords. The overture keyword selector tool, http://inventory.overture.com/d/searchinventory/suggestion/, is another very helpful tool. Unlike Google, you enter your keyword phrase and it will show you the number of searches conducted for that phrase as well as a selection of relevant phrases.

Now if you only see one or two hundred, then that is your market and maybe you might want to rethink your subject matter. It all depends on how much money you'd like to make on your book.

On the other hand, if you see ten or twenty thousand, then you know that this is a topic that people are interested in. (It may also be a saturated market, in which case you may want to more finely tune your subject matter to a highly targeted niche or consider another topic.)

Using these keyword tools, you might also want to start thinking about the title of your book. Using the diabetes example, you might want to search possible titles like "30 Days to Reversing Diabetes For Good!" I don't know if it is really possible to reverse diabetes in 30 days but it is a niche topic, and if you can back up your claims with evidence, then the world would be a better place.

Seek out a niche. Let's say that you're an avid rock climber and you want to write and market a book on rock climbing, but you're not sure what specific part of rock climbing you should write about or which topic would have the most demand.

Here's how to break it down:

1. **Look for a need.** Maybe there are 100 books on how to learn to rock climb, but not very many books, or maybe none at all, which focus on how to rock climb with children. There's a potential need.

2. **Talk to people with similar interests.** Talk to other climbers and experts in the field and find out what they want to know more about or questions that they're often asked.

3. **Consult with friends, family, and associates.** You can approach this two ways. You can come up with a list of potential topics and present your list to your friends, family and associates and have them choose the most intriguing topic.

OR

You can ask your friends, family, and associates to write down five topics that they'd most like to read about. Use the list to generate ideas from your bank of knowledge.

How To Write A Guaranteed Best Seller!

In one sentence, bestsellers are books that solve people's problems.

Whether a person needs tips on how to improve their love life, how to make millions of dollars, or how to clean their bathrooms with environmentally safe products, your book should help people solve their problems.

One of the most common formats for this popular type of non-fiction book is the "How To."

It is also one of the simplest to write.

"How To" books are written in an easy to read conversational tone. They're often broken up into step-by-step chapters or easy to contain sections. This makes it easier for you, as the writer, to organize your thoughts on each individual topic. It also makes the books easy to read, which is one of the reasons why they're so popular.

When You're Choosing Your Book's Topic, Draft A Sales Letter First To Make Sure That It Will Work.

Why write your sales letter first?

Your sales letter begins with a catchy headline. The number one benefit that readers will gain from reading your book. If you can't come up with a benefit, then you don't have a good topic.

Your sales letter will address additional benefits, needs and solutions, again if you cannot provide a full sales letter highlighting all of the benefits your book will provide then you don't have a book.

How To Write A Winning Sales Letter

I should mention that you can hire people to write sales copy for you. If you're not interested in writing sales material, then check online freelance websites where you can hire a writer to write a sales page for your book. (You can also hire people to review your book at these sites.) However, you are a writer and you know your book better than anyone does, so you are certainly qualified to write the sales copy. Besides, how else will you know if you have a book topic worthy of selling if you can't sell it first!

Actually, writing sales copy can be relatively easy and very fun.

Sales copy is composed of five key components:

1.   A headline that attracts attention
2.   The statement of a problem that needs to be solved
3.   A solution to the problem and copy to support why your book solves their problem
4.   A call to action
5.   Testimonials and reviews

How to Write a Profitable Headline

Headlines are critical to your sales copy. In fact, according to many experts, it is the most important element of your sales piece. There is a great deal of competition for your prospect's time—you need to catch your reader's attention immediately.

Your headline has many tasks, including getting your prospect's attention, drawing the reader into your copy, and defining your message - all with less than 15 words.

There are some basic considerations when writing your headline.

•   Who is your targeted reader?

- What problem are you solving for them?
- What emotions are triggered by this problem?
- What are the important features of your book?
- Lastly, why would your customer want to buy your book?

Write your headline as if you were creating short, curiosity-arousing tease copy on an outer envelope. Compel your recipients to read further without being so blatant in your promotion that it turns them off.

Learn How to Eat Away Arthritis.

Notice how it piques the reader's curiosity? Eat away arthritis? What are they talking about? Maybe I'll read on.

Now you've got them reading your message. Provided you can pull your reader effectively through your copy all the while selling your book you've done what you set out to do.

Here are ten ways to produce effective headlines:

1. State a benefit.

2. Use descriptive words that help the reader visualize.

3. Highlight your offer in your headline.

4. Use numbers and statistics.

5. Make it newsworthy using words like new, introducing, or announcing.

6. Stress your guarantee.

7. Make a big promise. This is used a lot: "Lose 20 pounds in 20 days."

8. Use a "reasons why" headline. "10 reasons why you're losing money in the stock market."

9. Anticipate and address your prospect's fears.

10. Pique their curiosity.

There are of course many ways to produce a good, attention-getting headline.

Psychologists and skilled copywriters will both tell

you that people don't buy for logical reasons. They buy for emotional ones. Fear, greed, curiosity, benevolence, jealousy, lust, insecurity, pride, and frustration are among some of the effective emotions copywriters tap into.

By using emotion to create a need or desire in your headline, you spur the reader into action. Of course, the next step is solving their need or desire by offering them your book and backing up their emotional decision with a logical one.

When writing your headline, it is often useful to write several headlines and choose the most effective one, or to write your copy first and let your copy dictate the headline.

Regardless of how you proceed, experience and reading other eye-catching headlines will help you craft powerful headlines.

Here are some examples of powerful headlines designed to sell books:

- "Rich Dad, Poor Dad: What the Rich Teach Their Kids About Money--That the Poor and Middle Class Do Not!"
- "How to Make Your Catering Facility Virtually Competition Proof"
- How To Eat Away Arthritis. Gain Relief from the pain and discomfort of arthritis through nature's remedies.

Don't Forget to Appeal to Your Prospect's Emotions

By using emotion to create a need or desire that your book can fulfill, you spur the reader into action. You create the need by tapping into the emotion of your reader and then you solve their need by offering them your book as a solution. Of course, this is after you've provided them legitimate reasons why your book is the solution.

Testimonials and Reviews. How to Obtain Them and How to Use Them on The Back of Your Book, Website, Direct Mail Copy, and Your Press Package.

There are magazines and companies that review books specifically for authors and I have included a list of these resources in this book. Additionally, you can ask experts in the industry related to your book if they will write a review. They don't need to read the entire book; you can send them a few chapters or a galley. Also, don't be afraid to ask associates for a review.

Reviews and testimonials are worth 100 perfectly written sales pages. They are the proof that your book is worth the money. Testimonials are one of the 'back up' sources of credibility in your sales copy.

Of course, when you're just starting out, you don't have any testimonials.

However, there is an easy solution to that dilemma. Quality, reputable testimonials can be obtained by sending your book to a dozen associates and asking for their opinion. In fact, if you trade a testimonial for a link to his or her website, then I cannot imagine anyone saying no to your request.

Why are reviews and testimonials important?

- Testimonials are one thousand times more powerful than you blowing your own horn. People tend to believe 2nd party testimonials more than if you say how good your book is.
- Testimonials help prospects feel more secure about their purchase
- Testimonials, if written well, can address prospects concerns.
- Reviews add credibility to your book. Prospects see that your book has helped others.

Once you have a couple of beneficial testimonials from

associates, add them to your sales letter, landing page and press kit, and then go about collecting some more.

How to Make your Book Stand Above Your Competition.

1. Buy 5 to10 of your competitor's books. Go through them and compile a list of the benefits they offer. Meet a need that isn't addressed by your competition.

2. Track the contents of each competitor's book. Return to your book plan and make sure that you cover all of their information and then add some of your own unique information.

3. Add something proprietary. The best and easiest way to add a unique and proprietary aspect to your book is to create an acronym and use it to the benefit of your readers, for example: BRWT Force. Brain Rush Writing Technique.

   The process is proven and it works, I simply created the acronym to make the process proprietary and beneficial to my readers. You can do this too.

4. Provide your readers tools that your competition doesn't. In addition to an acronym or two, you can include useful tools that your readers will benefit from. For example, some books come with workbook pages, recipes, blueprints, buyer's guide, resource information, and even a CD or simple software product. Each tool should be designed to help your reader and offer them a unique benefit. Additionally, you can use these add on tools to build a whole sales funnel of products you can provide your readers to keep the demand for your information high and your profits even higher.

Assuming that you've put together an award winning book, you have winning subject matter, and are offering amazing benefits to your readers, how do you make sure your potential readers choose you over the competition? What makes one book stand out above the rest?

BEST SELLERS ARE IN THE PACKAGING.

You can have the absolute best book on the planet. It can solve the world's problems and provide the secret to life but if no one notices it, it won't do anyone, including you, any good.

So how do you get your book noticed?

It's all in the packaging. Really, it is. Would you buy a candy bar in a brown paper wrapper? Or would you buy a candy bar with a yummy clever name and a picture of the candy bar on the shiny outside wrapper?

The one in the brown paper wrapper may actually frighten you, right? It will seem suspect and perhaps even perceived as tasting bad before you taste it, even if it is the same candy bar. This kind of taste test or packing test has been performed hundreds of times and the result is the same. People perceive the item, regardless of what it is, to be better if it is in an appealing package. Conversely, people perceive things to be bad if they are wrapped in an unappealing package.

This holds true for books too. In fact, a book buying decision is made in twenty seconds. What on earth can a person determine about your book in twenty seconds? What are they looking at? What are they basing their decision on?

1. Book title

2. Color of front cover

3. Graphics on front cover

4. Author's name and credentials

That's it. Those four items play an extremely crucial role in your potential reader's buying decision.

I'm going to address them briefly here and go into more depth about them in Chapter Four.

1. Book Title and Sub Title. Your book title has a big job. It needs to attract interest, it needs to incite curiosity, it needs to make a big promise, it needs to have credibility, and it needs to do all of this without sounding ridiculous—it needs to be believable. A lot of this can be accomplished by adding a sub title to your book. In fact, I believe that no book should be without a subtitle. Let's look at the title "Eat Away Arthritis." That alone does attract curiosity and interest; it even gives a big promise. What it doesn't completely do is provide credibility or believability.

2. That's where the sub title comes in handy. "Gain relief from the pain and discomfort of arthritis through nature's remedies." This provides credibility and believability. Now the reader knows exactly how they're to eat away arthritis and they know the benefit of the book.

3. Colors set the mood for your book. They attract interest and set the mood for the book. For example, the eating away arthritis book would sell better if the cover were to have natural colors, the colors of food. If it's red and black, it's likely to give readers the wrong mood/ impression of your book. On the other hand, if you have a book about making millions before your 25 then you don't want calm neutral colors; you want strong powerful colors that attract attention and demand money and power. If you are not comfortable with the graphic design aspect of your book, you can consult with your printer or consider hiring an expert through an outsourcing service like elance.

4. Images/graphics. Like the colors of your book, you also need to take a look at the images that are represented on your cover. Would you put a picture of an old, arthritic person on your Eating Away Arthritis book cover or pictures of tasty, healthy foods? The answer is obvious.

Remember to not go overboard with the graphics, they should be the background. You want people to notice the title and subtitle first and foremost. The rest is just mood setting.

5. Author's name. Your name, of course, should be on the cover. Additionally, you should include any credentials that you have that are relevant to your book. The arthritis book is written by a naturopathic physician and she includes her credentials after her name because they are extremely relevant. Additionally, if you don't have initial credentials, you can simply state your credentials. If you wrote a book on breeding poodles, you can write John Smith, AKA Standard Poodle breeder for more than 20 years. The point is to add credibility to your content.

6. So now your reader has made a quick decision about their level of interest in your book. What do they do once they've decided that they're interested in your book? They turn it over and read the back. If they're shopping online, they look at your table of contents and they scroll down to read reviews of your book. It's all part of the packaging! Well take a look at how to format the back of your book and table of contents in our next section.

Laughter is the best medicine.

– Origin Unknown

Chapter 4

Getting Out Of The Garage And Onto The Street

SIMPLE STEPS TO GET YOUR BOOK PUBLISHED

WHY SELF-PUBLISHING IS THE BEST CHOICE.

Self-publishing is the number one best thing you can do for your life and your career. Notice that I put life before career.

Why?

You know all the reasons that you want to write a book: money, prestige, satisfaction, sharing your specialized knowledge and 97 other reasons.

Self-publishing is a guarantee that these things will happen.

Publishing via traditional means i.e. publishing houses, is an endlessly frustrating experience. It involves hours of work creating a book proposal. Hours of work crafting query letters to agents and then waiting days, weeks, months, and even years receiving rejection letters in the mail. Often times your material hasn't even been read!

None of this means you don't have a book worthy of being published; it means simply that you're communicating with the wrong people.

Self-publishing is your direct route to the right people, your reader and your customer!

You are guaranteed publication! There is no better way to do it.

Self publication means more money.

Let's assume you do go the traditional publishing route for your first book. If you were able to receive an advance of 6-10 thousand dollars.

Your literary agent will take 15% off the top.

Generally speaking, hardcover books pay royalty rates of 10% on the first one to 250,000 copies sold. So if your book has a cover price of $25.00, then you will earn a $2.50 royalty on every copy sold, up to 250,000 copies.

This means that if you only sell 10,000 copies, then you will only earn $25,000. Keep in mind that your agent gets 15% of this too, and all of this is paid after you've earned your advance. Paperback royalties pay an average of 6%.

And some publishing contracts even stipulate that if your book doesn't earn back its advance, you owe them!

In addition to that, publishers can withhold your royalties as a reserve against book returns and you're still responsible for promoting your own book, which can mean hiring a publicist. There goes your advance!

So....if you're willing to do the legwork yourself, meaning packaging, printing, distributing, and promoting your book, every single cent from every single sale goes directly into your pocket. So if you sell 1000 books at 19.99 each, you've made $19,990. That's three times what you'd make if you had sold it to a publishing house.

Of course you do have to cover your printing and marketing costs but you'll earn significantly more per book and with proper packaging, you can roll your costs into the price of your book. For example, if your book costs $2.00 to print and market then you up your price to $21.99. Readers will be willing to pay the extra $2.00 because you've told them, through your amazing packaging, that the book will benefit their lives the way no other book can.

In fact, I've seen books sell for several hundred dollars. If you have extremely specialized and unique knowledge, you can price it at any level that you desire and people will buy it.

Don't lose control. Why self-publishing leaves the most important decisions up to you.

Did you know that 60% of publishers do not give you final approval on copyediting?

WHAT?

It's your book. Your name is going on it, right? Your reputation, your satisfaction and your pride. OF course you should have final say.

But it gets worse...

23% don't give you the right to choose your title or cover design. And more than 1/3 don't involve you in the book's promotion.

YOU HAVE NO CONTROL with a publishing house.

I don't know about you but I find this appalling. How are you supposed to profit from your book if you have no say? Presumably you know your market better than the publishers because you are your market.

Self-publishing gives you 100% control. You make the decisions about your book. Now that doesn't mean that you can't seek guidance from experienced publishers. Many publish or print on demand companies offer valuable guidance with cover design and typesetting, but ultimately the final decision is yours to make.

I'm sure some people are more comfortable giving others control but I guarantee that allowing others to make your decisions will leave you frustrated and unsatisfied. Besides, you're not one of those people. You love being in control of your life.

Self-publishing means immediate satisfaction.

Traditional publishing works like this:

- You send your book proposal to an agent.
- You wait 1 to 3 months for a response.
- You receive a rejection.

- You send your proposal to another agent.
- You wait another 1-3 months.
- You receive a rejection.

This process will repeat many times!

- You get an agent.
- Your agent sends your book proposal and/or manuscript to a publisher.
- You wait 3 or more months.
- You receive a rejection.
- Your agent sends your book proposal and/or manuscript to another publisher
- You wait
- You receive a rejection.

This too will repeat many times.

Now let's assume that you receive a contract, which based on the number of submissions agents and publishers receive each year compared to the number of books actually published means that you have less than 1% chance of doing this. Did you know that publishers generally run on an 18 month publishing schedule? It's true, it's built into their production cycle. This means that after you've accomplished all of the required re-writes, it will still take 18 months to get your book on the bookstore shelves.

What if you're writing on a timely topic? What are the odds that it is still going to be timely 2 years after you initially wrote it.

Self-publishing is super fast. In fact, I've known people to have a copy of their printed book 2 weeks after they've finished writing it!

Imagine the power you'll have over your competitors if your book comes out 2 years before theirs!

More reasons to self-publish: (As if you need more reasons)

- You become a business owner/publisher

- You get the tax advantages of being a business owner
- You set your own writing and publishing schedule
- You can update and modify your book easily any time you choose
- You can publish any type of content.
- Self-publishing has a long standing history. In fact, 78% of books sold come from small and self-publishers. Self-publishing is a viable means of publishing. Mark Twain, Richard Nixon, L.Ron Hubbard, John Grisham, Henry David Thoreau, and even Edgar Allen Poe have self-published.
- You might be familiar with these self-published book titles: "What Color is Your Parachute?", "The Celestine Prophecy", "The One Minute Manager", and most recently the children's fiction book "Eragon" which was picked up by a major publisher. The movie rights were sold and the young author is well on his way to fortune and fame.
- Lastly, self-publishing often leads to large publishing contracts. If your book sells well as a self-published book traditional houses will be banging down your door to purchase your book. Then you will be able to negotiate more money and more control in your contract!

The Future Of Self-publishing

Did you know that more than 60% of all books are bought in non-bookstore establishments?

Where is everyone buying their books?

Online

People, thanks to the internet, have become accustomed to

instant information and instant gratification. In fact, many self-published authors offer their books in electronic form, books, as well as a printed book.

Let's go back and discuss instant gratification. Are you familiar with the one click option on Amazon? With an easy click of your mouse your book is on its way. You don't have to enter your address or credit card info, it's already entered. You don't have to choose shipping options.

One click and your book will be in your mailbox in as little as three days. Ordering is easy and painless and thanks to shopping cart software advances and advances in distribution services, it's only going to get easier.

Why drive all the way to the bookstore when all you have to do is click a button while sitting on your couch watching LOST and the book is in your hands before the end of the week?

Or even better, the book is downloaded onto your computer instantly and you're reading it during the commercials!

We are a multitasking society that is accustomed to instant gratification. As a publisher, if you don't take advantage of this by making your book easily accessible and available and by marketing and packaging it well, you're missing out on thousands of dollars.

Technological advances mean more money in your pocket as well. As of March 2007, Google has digitized more than 1 million books. For the consumer, this means the ability to read complete copies of public domain books, but it also means that consumers can read your table of contents, introduction, and even a sample chapter should you choose to market your book this way.

Many feel that Google is infringing on copyright laws by digitizing this information, however as a publisher, you can take advantage of it and make portions of your book available to your potential readers. If they like what they see, which of course they will, then they'll buy your book.

Time will tell the future of Google Books, but self-publishing is here to stay!

Amazon has even recognized the rapidly growing trend and offers their own POD service called BookSurge.

POD companies and book distributors as well as subsidiary markets like website developers for self-publishers are popping up everywhere.

Because there is tons of money to be made in self-publishing and self-publishers have needs too!

WHY BOOKSTORES ARE THE WORST PLACE TO SELL BOOKS

Books are more commonly sold in:

- Stores with relevant products
- Catalogs
- Online

According to American booksellers association, bookstore sales are steadily decreasing yet the number of books sold is increasing. How is this happening?

Most people enter a bookstore looking for a specific book. They've already made their buying decision and there is very little that you can do to attract their attention and make a sale.

The rest of bookstore visitors are browsers. They have very little or no intention of actually buying a book.

It is very difficult to target your market in a large bookstore where bindings are stacked on top of each other and there is very little to differentiate your binding from your competitors other than the title of your book.

This isn't to say that you shouldn't place your book in traditional brick and mortar stores, but know that you'll receive only about 35% of the profit from each sale and the majority of your sales will come from other sources and online sales.

How and where to sell your self-published book online:

1. Amazon —There are three ways to place your book on Amazon.com.

   You can join their Advantage Program. This program allows you to use their service to sell and distribute your book. There's an annual fee, $30 at the time this book was written, and they take a percentage from every sale of 55%.

You can also participate in their Pro-Merchant program. This allows you to sell a large volume through their marketplace service. I don't recommend this for your self published book. This is better for auction type items or stores.

2. You can also list your book with a distributor, like Ingram and a listing will automatically be created for you on Amazon.com, which you can then edit and expand upon.

3. Your own website. I go into detail about how to do this in the last section of this book.

4. Other websites with relevant information and products. For example, selling a pet training book at PetSmart or your local pet store's site. That way they can carry your book in store too.

BOOK PRODUCTION

The second task to self-publishing is actually making a book out of your manuscript.

You will have to make the following decisions:

- Cover design
- Internal artwork and layout
- Font, for example, Times New Roman or Arial
- Type of binding, for example, spiral, ring, stitched, perfect, etc.
- Hardcover or softcover
- Book size (standard book size is 5.5" by 8.5")
- Type of paper book is printed on
- Color or black and white

- Number of pages. It is generally easier for consumers to justify a book purchase if the book is over 100 pages.

Your printer can help you with a majority of these decisions by offering suggestions and examples. You can also visit bookstores and find books that you want to model.

OPTIONS FOR PRINTING YOUR BOOK

There seems to be some confusion around the world about Print On Demand. This is because the field is ever evolving. There used to be a very unfortunate reputation to a majority of POD publishers, but thanks to ever changing policies and standards, there are some viable options for you. Let's begin by drawing an invisible line between Print On Demand Publishers and Print On Demand Printers.

POD PUBLISHERS

Unlike POD printers, POD publishers may provide extra services like designing a book cover, editing your book, and obtaining an ISBN number. They can be a good option if you need less than 50 books because the price is generally lower than what you would pay for a POD printer. However, make sure that you read your contract carefully and that you fully investigate the POD publisher that you are considering. Some publishers require exclusive rights to your book.

POD PRINTERS

POD printers are just that, printers. They do not invest in your product. They simply manufacture it. The cost can be a bit expensive and generally ranges from $5 to $10 per book, depending on your book's specifics. POD printers can be a good and cost effective option if your book is nearing the end of its life yet you still have the occasional order trickling in. This way you can order one book at a time and it eliminates the possible expense of having to keep an inventory on hand. The print quality is usually good. Again, as with any company, read your contract carefully and make sure to investigate the company.

DIGITAL PRINTERS PQN, PRINT QUALITY NEEDED

This is a good option for the author that needs fewer than 2500 copies. It is cost effective, the print quality is good, and it normally takes less than two weeks to print.

OFFSET PRINTERS.

When you need more than 2500 books, your best choice is offset printing. The cost will equate to about $1.25 per book for about 3000 books. However, the more books that you print, the less expensive your cost will be.

TIP: Consider your storage and distribution options as well as your sales goals before you order 10,000 copies of your book. Also, according to Author's Guild a book is judged to be successful once it sells 7,500 copies. Keep that number in mind when making your printing decisions.

POD RESOURCES:

- Profits Publishing http://profitspublishing.com/
- Authorhouse http://www.authorhouse.com
- Infinity Publishing http://www.infinitypublishing.com
- Trafford Publishing http://www.trafford.com
- iUniverse http://www.iUniverse.com
- Xlibris http://www.xlibris.com

MAKING YOUR DISTRIBUTION AND ORDER FULFILLMENT DECISIONS

The next thing that you'll need to handle as a self-publisher is the task of distribution. It may actually be to your benefit to hire a distributor; however, most distributors take 65% of the profit. A distributor's main purpose is to "sell" your book to bookstores and specialty stores.

Distributors also are able to sell your book to larger chain stores like Borders and Barnes and Noble. This can be to your benefit because it means that your exposure is much larger than sticking with smaller booksellers and specialty stores.

Also, consider contracting with a library wholesaler. Libraries purchase 90% of their inventory from wholesalers.

Amazon.com offers an Advantage program for self-publishing distribution via their website. For more information, you can visit:

http://advantage.amazon.com/gp/vendor/public/join-advantagbooks

Barnes and Noble offers a similar program, which can be found at: http://www.barnesandnoble.com/help/cds2.asp?PID =8148&linkid=9&z=y&cds2Pid=9481

BOOKSTORE DISTRIBUTOR RESOURCES

* Bookstore Distributors, for self-publishers
* Baker and Taylor http://www.btol.com/
* AMS http://www.advmkt.com
* Austin & Company http://www.austinandcompanyinc.com
* Biblio Distribution http://www.bibliodistribution.com
* Client Distribution Services http://www.cdsbooks.com
* National Book Network http://www.nbnbooks.com

- Publisher's Marketing Association http://www. pmaonline.org
- Rights & Distribution, Inc http://www.fellpub.com
- SCB Distributors http://www.scbdistributors.com

POD PRINTERS:

LighteningSource/Ingram Book Group http://www. lighteningsource.com

BookSurge, LLC http://www.booksurge.com

ORDER FULFILLMENT

Your final task as a self-published author is to fulfill orders that are placed.

You will need to decide how you are going to take orders by phone, fax, email, web store, snail mail, or all of the above. Do you accept credit cards? How will you ship? How will you take returns, if at all? Mail order purchasing is an easy and efficient process once you have established a routine. However, shipping individual books can be expensive. Will you charge for shipping? Where will you store the books?

POD Printers like LightningSource and POD Publishers like Profits Publishing include distribution and fulfillment services for their customers. (Note that they do not, however, market your book.)

You'll also have to establish the accounts receivable portion of your bookkeeping to make sure that all income is recorded properly. I recommend consulting with an accountant prior to establishing your business. An accountant can answer valuable questions about what business organization best fits your needs. They can also recommend methods for recording your sales and expenses and how to prepare for tax season.

I have had the same accountant for almost 3 decades. A good accountant won't cost you money they will save you money. Run your new book venture by a trusted accountant and set yourself up right from the first day.

There are of course several other tasks that you'll have to consider when setting up your publishing business:

SETTING UP YOUR PUBLISHING COMPANY

The first thing that you will need to do, once your book is written, is to start your own publishing company. To accomplish this you will first need to decide on a name for your company. Experts recommend against placing your name in the title of the company because it makes you look like a beginner. Additionally, do you really want your name listed as both the author and the publisher?

Rock Climbing With Children by Annette Smith

Copyright 2007, Annette Smith Publishing

The second thing that you will need to do is to choose a business structure and register your business. A business structure can be as basic as a self-proprietorship. Alternatively, you can choose a corporation if you are looking for more tax savings. Check with an attorney or an accountant if you have questions about what each means to you financially.

You'll also need to decide how you want to finance your business, what office equipment you need, and where you want to do business. This doesn't have to be too involved. You can operate on as small or large of a budget as you desire. Honestly, a computer is all you really need.

PRICING YOUR BOOK

Before you begin promotion, you'll also want to determine how much to charge for your book. The general rule of thumb is to charge 8 times what it cost you to produce it. Therefore, if it cost you $5 to produce the book, you'll charge $40. However, you want to consider your market and how much they'll be willing to pay for your book. It could be more or less than $40.

Additionally, you'll want to consider how you plan on promoting your book. If, for example, you want to incorporate a direct marketing campaign, you'll want to mark the book up slightly so that you can offer it at a discount.

BEFORE YOU'RE READY TO TAKE THE STEPS NECESSARY TO PROMOTE YOUR BOOK, YOU NEED TO CONSIDER A FEW FORMALITIES.

- ISBN numbers. An ISBN number isn't a requirement to sell a book yourself but it'll make it easier to record your book with booksellers and it is a formal registration process that signifies that you are in fact a publisher. In short, it makes you look more professional. Additionally, most booksellers like Amazon, require an ISBN number.

- Visit the ISBN website, http://www.isbn.org/ standards/home/isbn/us/secureapp.asp

- Fill out the application. Your initial cost will be over $250.00 for registration as a publisher and 10 ISBN numbers and I've been told that it can take more than 15 days to process, so have patience.

- Library of Congress Number. This is a number that is assigned by the Library of Congress to a book. It can also be referred to as the Preassigned Control Number or PCN. Numbers are only assigned to books that will be added to the library. You can apply for a number by visiting http://www.copyright.gov. Complete the application and then file for a number.

- Copyright Registration. The first step in registering your book is to print a copyright notice on your copyright page, usually the back of your title page. Your second step is to publish your book. Last, you'll want to visit http://www.loc.gov/copyright/forms to register your book.

Why Is Packaging So Important To Your Book Sales?

First impressions are extremely important. In fact, a buying decision is usually made in less than 20 seconds.

What can your prospect glean in 20 seconds about your book?

- Benefits
- Authority/Authors Name
- Design
- Content

All of this is gleaned from 4 key ingredients.

1. Title and Subtitle
2. Front Cover
3. Back Cover
4. Table of Contents

Let's address each, one at a time.

Your book's title is at least ½ of the buying decision. In it, your prospect will decide immediately if there is any benefit for them. They'll also make a snap judgment about the quality of the contents.

How do you choose a book? Chances are your attention is captured by a title, and the promise or benefit it delivers.

Let's take a look at an example Book Title:

'How To Train Your Dog'

Add compelling and powerful words to appeal to your reader's needs, hopes, and desires.

'How To Train Your Dog To Be The Most Obedient Dog On The Planet'

Now add a subheading to create an even more powerful and emotional title.

'Discover 99 Simple Secrets You Can Take Today To Create A Loyal,
Happy And Well Behaved Companion'

Now make sure that ALL of your words are compelling, active, and positive. In the subheading I would eliminate the word 'can' and change it to 'must'

Here's the final title:

How To Train Your Dog To Be The Most Obedient Dog OOn The Planet

Discover 99 Simple Secrets You Must Take Today
To Create A Loyal, Happy, And Well Behaved Companion.

Don't just tell them what information is in your book; tell them how they will benefit from the information in your book. How your book will meet their information needs and change their lives.

Take a look at your competitor's titles. How do they sell the benefits? What can you do better? What need or needs are they not fulfilling or addressing. Often you can come up with a winning title and sales letter first and the book contents follows naturally.

In addition to the title on the cover page, you're likely also attracted to the colors and graphics on the cover. Colors are mood triggers and the mood needs to fit your subject matter.

Graphics, to a lesser extent, are also used to attract attention.

Now turn your book over. What do you see?

Testimonials and reviews? A summary of the story or contents?

Non-fiction books are best presented with a bulleted list of benefits you'll receive from reading the book, a quick subject summary, and testimonials and endorsements from celebrities in the know. Grab a non-fiction book from your collection. Take a look at the back and what do you see? I've grabbed a book called Winner's Guide To Texas Hold'em Poker. A Smart Player's Guide To Winning at Hold'em.

On the back it says in big bold letters--Be a Winner At Texas Hold'em.

There's the benefit from reading this book. I immediately assume that when I'm done, I'll know how to win the game.

The back page headline is then followed by a few compelling paragraphs telling me that I'll learn step by step ways to win, that I'm learning from a pro, and that I will become a confident and proficient player if I read this book.

Of course there are a few well placed testimonials on the back too, just in case I need a bit more convincing.

Fiction books do it too. Fiction books are best sold with an active summary about the book's plot and a compelling hook at the end. Grab a fiction book or two from your collection and take a look at the back. What do you see? It's often called the elevator pitch; it is the very condensed and compelling summary of your book's plot and characters. You'll also find a few well placed reviews.

Here is a quick brief on how and where to get reviews for your book:

Send a chapter to one or all of the following magazines and book reviewers:

- Bookselling this week http://www.bookweb.org
- Foreword Magazine http://www.forewordmagazine. com
- Kirkus Reviews http://www.kirkusreviews.com
- Publisher's weekly http://www.publishersweekly.com
- Midwest Book Review http://www.midwestbookreview. com
- New York Review of Books http://www.nybooks.com
- Washington Post Book World http://www. washingtonpost.com

Send a chapter to a celebrity or expert in your subject matter. You can even be so bold as to send the testimonial hand written, a week or two after you've sent the chapter and requested a testimonial, and simply ask them to sign it.

Lastly, you can send a chapter to associates and request a testimonial. Be sure to follow up all testimonials and reviews with a thank you!

In addition to the front and back cover of your book, there is one more key ingredient to a winning book package.

YOUR TABLE OF CONTENTS IS YOUR NUMBER 1 OPPORTUNITY TO SHOW YOUR READERS EVERYTHING THAT THEY WILL GAIN FROM READING YOUR BOOK.

It is your opportunity to demonstrate that the cost of your book is a steal and it is your best opportunity to engage their curiosity. After reading your table of contents, readers should feel that they MUST read your book.

How do you accomplish all of this in a little old table of contents?

You utilize the concept of Direct Response Marketing (Define)

- You use emotions
- Benefits
- Call to action
- Powerful headlines

Let's now take a look at a chapter within a book and how to name it. Using the dog training book example let's assume that the first chapter of the book is about welcoming your new puppy into your home.

Now that's a fine enough title but it can become more compelling with a little adjustment. Let's add a subtitle to the chapter's title. "10 things you can do today to set the tone."

It breaks the chapter down into measurable action steps and it engages the reader. Now they must buy the book because they need to find out what to do with their puppy the very first day to make all subsequent days easier and more fulfilling.

Again, if you change the word 'can' to must or have to or should then it makes the information more urgent and active.

Add 'for the rest of your dog's life' and it becomes even more compelling and triggers the reader's emotions to bond with their dog.

Here's the final title for Chapter One:

Welcoming Your New Puppy Home

10 Things You Must Do Today To Set The Tone For The Rest Of Your Dog's Life.

Remember, your reader is going to have access to your Table of Contents, it's a marketing tool, so it is important to put some time and energy into your chapter titles. It's your package, your sales pitch.

Direct Marketing/Copy Writing Resources

- Direct Marketing Association http://www.www.the-dma.org
- Gale Group http://www.galegroup.com
- The Writer, Inc http://www.writermag.com
- Writer's Digest Books http://www.writersdigest.com

You can't win if you don't try!

- Robert H .Schwaninger Jr., law firm of Brown and Schwaninger

Chapter 5

Winning The Blue Ribbon

SIMPLE STEPS FOR A BESTSELLER

PROMOTING YOUR BOOK

Initially, promoting your book can be a time consuming effort. You should expect to devote 20 hours a week in the very beginning, to promoting your book. This is a bare minimum. It can actually require much more time depending on your promotion decisions and money making goals. Remember, according to the American Publishers Association in order to be considered successful, a non-fiction book must sell 7,500 copies; a fiction book must sell 5000 copies.

One famous quote is that "being an author is 5% writing and 95% promotion."

Don't get discouraged by this number! Once your initial promotions have been effective, the momentum will carry your book sales forward and you'll have to devote much less time on your sales and marketing and can spend more time looking forward to your next book or information product.

Note that if your goal is to be on the Amazon bestseller's

list, then Amazon actually calculates their 100 best sellers hourly. So if a book promotion turns into 100 sales on Amazon in one day, then you'll very likely make it very high on the list. Consider then when you're planning your book promotions. You can time an email and offer a limited promotion to spur a large volume of sales in a short amount of time.

However, you're not just reaping the monetary benefits from selling your book, you're increasing the number of opportunities that will be presented to you because you are a published author. You'll get new clients, you'll be invited to speak, host a show, and entertain at parties.

You're the expert and if you don't sell 7,500 copies of your book, don't worry! You're still taking huge steps in improving the quality of your life and the lives of the people that you touch through the publication of your book. If you ask me, that's the definition of success!

Let's take a look at some ways that you can promote your book!

Promotion options include:

- Advertising
- Press releases
- Articles
- Book signings
- Book reviews
- Radio and talk shows
- Community events and organizations
- Website
- Blog

I will address each briefly here and we will revisit many of the same promotion tools in depth in the chapter on books. Let's begin with advertising.

Advertising can be extremely expensive and your cost per sale may be more than the medium is worth. For example, if you take out a half page advertisement in a national magazine, presumably somewhat affiliated with your book's subject matter, then the cost can range from $1,000 to $5,000. The odds are good that the sales the advertisement generates will not equal the cost of the ad.

However, advertisements can be beneficial for gaining attention, if not leading directly to a sale. You can also consider buying ad space online with blogs or other websites that have a similar theme or subject matter as your book. Then all it takes is a click onto your website and a potential sale is made. Additionally, web advertisements can be much less expensive than print advertisements.

Articles are a terrific way to gain credibility and attention for your book. You can query online and print publications with article ideas. You can write for businesses and organizations that share a similar subject matter. For example, if your book is about youth basketball coaching, then you could contact coaching associations to see if they're interested in including an article in their newsletter about dealing with difficult parents or motivating young players.

Online Articles

The next great form of content to drive customers to your website is the free article websites.

Articles that are made available on free websites are an amazing way to drive traffic to your website. Posted articles are read by visitors, who then click to your website for more information. The articles are posted on blogs, which leads to increased website traffic. The articles are also reprinted in newsletters and on other websites, which provides traffic. It also provides links to your site, which in turn can increase your website ranking with the search engines.

There are literally thousands of article websites. Here are some of my favorites:

- http://ezinearticles.com
- http://www.goarticles.com
- http://www.articledashboard.com/
- http://www.articlefinders.com/
- http://www.articlefinders.com/
- http://www.ideamarketers.com/
- http://www.articlealley.com/
- http://www.articledepot.co.uk/
- http://www.certificate.net/
- http://www.amazines.com/

The key to publishing articles on these sites is to make sure that you first provide valuable content and that you provide at least one link to your website. You should also include a short bio with a way to contact you for more information.

We'll talk more about what to do with your website visitors in a bit, for now just know that driving traffic to your website is only the beginning. Once they're there you have to capture their email address.

The great thing is that you already have a source for all of the content to provide to these websites – your book! Website articles are generally 500 words or so. All you have to do is pull a section from your book on a specific topic, format it for an article, and submit it to the article website. It's free, it's uncomplicated, and it drives traffic to your site, which means that it sells books!

How to Provide Informative Content That Will Attract Website Visitors

Most marketers know the value of providing free information to draw visitors to their website; however, where they often fall short is in the quality of the information that they provide. Their content falls flat and they don't get the website visitors that they were counting on.

Regardless of the format, it is important to create quality content for your readers. Failure to do so can result in the loss of a potential customer.

5 Tips To Craft Promotional Content

1. Stay on subject. This is simple. If your site is selling a book about weight loss, don't write an article about gardening. Instead, review health supplements, write an exercise guide, and give away free recipes.

   Ask yourself what your customers would want to know and then write about it. Alternatively, you can ask your customers for ideas and then listen. Chances are they'll give you a lot of useful information.

2. Keep your content focused, clear, and concise. Make it simple and only try to address one specific subject in each piece of copy. Copy that tries to address too many points often end up being messy and confusing. Often one main subject with three to five points is generally enough for a one or two page article or blog.

3. Make it readable. This means that if you're writing for online readers, then keep it short. Online readers often skim. Make sure there is lots of white space and formatting to keep it easy on the eyes. Underline, bold, numbers, and bullets all pull a reader's eye through the copy and highlight the key areas of interest.

4. Forget SEO optimization. Don't think about search engine optimization when you're writing your copy until you are finished. Make sure that you create a superb article or report, then go back and place your keywords and keyword phrases where they are appropriate. Copy that has been crafted around keywords usually feels forced and awkward.

5. Don't forget the power of your headline. Headlines make you or break you. Your headline, no matter what you're writing, needs to catch your reader's attention and draw them into the copy. There are of course

secrets to crafting catchy headlines some of which include:

- Asking a question – "Are you worried about your financial security?"
- Providing a "How To" – "How Lose 10 Pounds in 10 Days"
- The Command – "Increase Your Website Traffic Now!"

When you provide quality, informative content to your readers, they'll not only tell friends and family, but they'll come back for more. Webmasters will link to your content, blogs will post links to your content, and people will join your opt-in list.

The number of visitors to your website will increase, your lead list will grow, your customer list will multiply, and your bottom line will swell. It's a win-win situation and all it takes is a little time and effort.

COMMON ARTICLE WRITING MISTAKES

The following is a list of what not to do when writing articles to market your book.

- Avoid using jargon or tech speak. Each industry has its own language. However, people new to the industry will not be familiar with the language. Use jargon and you run the risk of alienating prospects before they've even had the opportunity to see what you have to offer. Additionally, articles that are written using words that people are unfamiliar with may make you seem condescending, and I'm sure that isn't how you want your potential customers to feel.

- Instead, write the article as if you were speaking to someone you just met at a social outing. Someone who has no idea who you are and what you do. Assume that person is of average intelligence and write in a conversational, friendly tone.

- The length of your article can also be a critical point. When writing for the Internet, an article that is too short runs the risk of being dismissed by readers and potential customers as not having much valuable content. An article that is too long overwhelms. Most people, while they spend a good amount of time at the computer, don't want to spend too much time reading a single article. A good rule of thumb for an article on the Internet is about 400 to 500 words for an article.

- When using the free article sites to draw business, you must not forget to include some sort of hook or selling piece in your article. For example, if you wrote a book on herbal supplements, then you could publish an article on the many causes of joint pain. The closing for your article might read like this,

While joint pain can be difficult to live with, there are options to both dealing with it and eliminating it all together. For more information on treatment options visit www.eliminatejointpainforever. com

Note that most article sites will not let you directly promote your book in your article. In fact, most will only allow a link in your bio or contact information box. You are not allowed to make any kind of offer or entice people to visit your website.

Always utilize the signature or bio box at the end of your article. This is an example of one that I use.

Bob Burnham, Entrepreneur, Consultant and Author of:

'101 Reasons Why You Must Write A Book'
For Your **FREE** MP3 (Value $97.00)
'How To Make A 6 Figure Income Writing & Publishing Your Own Book'

Go to: http://www.ExpertAuthorPublisher.com

Note that the anchor text link uses keywords that will help my site to optimize in the search engines.

If your reader likes your article and information it is likely they will click on your link for more information.

Generally, your article will be declined if you blatantly try to solicit business. The purpose of publishing on free article sites is simply to provide quality information and tell others where they can find more—at your website of course!

Now you have people visiting your site, purchasing products, and signing up to be on your mailing list. Leave your hook out and you're simply providing them with information for information's sake, and that probably won't be enough to sell your book or your other products.

Book reviews are not only a good way to promote your book but they're good copy for your website, press kit, and book covers. Prior to publishing your book, send a galley -- a pre-publication printed copy of your book usually bound and trimmed but may exclude cover art-- to reviewers. The big players are:

- Publisher's Weekly
- Library Journal
- Kirkus Reviews
- The New York Times Book Review
- The Los Angeles Times Magazine
- BookPage
- Quality Books, Inc.

Contact information for each of these companies is listed in our resources section. If you don't hear back from these companies after two months, send a follow up letter and consider sending a published copy of your book. Additionally, there are magazines that may review your book once it is published.

Blogs are an author's friend! Posting on blogs, your own and on other relevant blogs is a great way to promote your book. You're hitting a very targeted market when you blog and you're reaching potentially thousands of customers that will be interested in what you have to say.

Additionally, blogs are easy to do yourself and attach to your website. Additionally, remember those forums, newsgroups, and chat rooms that you visited when you were researching your book. Revisit them and promote your book. I know authors and copywriters that frequently post on a small business forum. They have made many sales and gained many customers based on their communications with others on this site.

Once again, you will find you will be frowned upon for any blatant advertising or even asked to leave the forum. However, in almost all cases you can put in your signature into the bio box or signature areas at the end of any article or information you contribute. Put together a good signature and get into the habit of using it every time you post anything.

Book signings are required whether you self-publish or publish via traditional means. The key to a book signing is to make it an event.

Book signings are a two-step process. Your first step is to set up your book signing with local bookstores. Contact any bookstore where you would like to hold signing. You will have to make a good sales pitch because signings cost bookstores money.

Attend conferences and trade shows that might have a similar subject matter. Again, you'll want to present your book and topic in the most exciting and interesting light possible to gain an opportunity to sell your book.

In addition to bookstores, you can contact organizations and associations that are affiliated with the topic of your book. If you wrote about pet training, then contact pet stores, animal hospitals, animal associations, human societies, etc.

You'll want to make your book signing as interesting as

possible. Do this by making it an event. Don't just expect to sit there and sign books. People won't approach you unless you're:

- 1. Famous
- 2. Interesting!
- 3. Giving away something for free

Give a talk on how your book or subject matter affects others. Give something away for free. You should tie your freebie into your book's topic if you can. For example, if you wrote a book on how to train your pet, then give away pet training clickers.

If you wrote a book on training dogs, then bring along your dog. Hand out dog treats for people to take home, and make sure that you have plenty of books to sign and sell!

The second step to your book signing is to let everyone that you have ever met or spoken to or corresponded with in your life know that you are having a book signing. This is where your email and contact list can come in very handy.

Send out a special postcard announcing your event. Include it in your newsletter. Offer the first 5, 10, 20 attendees something free. You can even offer them a free book! The more people that you're able to draw to the event, the more news it will make and the more word of mouth press you'll receive.

Radio and talk shows. Once you have a press kit (this will include a bio, a brief description of your book, its market, and your credentials), you can contact radio and talk show producers to see if they're interested in speaking with you.

Adult Education Classes This is virtually an untapped market for you to let people know about your book. Most Adult Education Schools are looking for people to instruct classes on any range of topics.

In most average size cities in North America you would be able to teach several night courses a month on your niche. This introduces people to you, your book and as always if done properly builds your customer list. If done properly it can be a very lucrative way of earning a full time income for just part time work.

You only have to submit a suggestion to a course by outline to the school and I have found from my experience they are very eager to have you teach at night. Not only are you getting paid to build your list, you can end up with some very profitable backend sales.

I highly recommend you look into buying Mike Round's video called:

Your Guide To Making Money Through The:
- **Rubber Band Circuit**
- **Rubber Chicken Circuit**
- **Radio Talk Show Circuit**

It's a 3 CD set that's very inexpensive and will help with your book, products or business. His website URL is:

http://www.rmacart.com/

Community events and organizations. Many community events and organizations are starving to get speakers. You can give anywhere from 20 minute to 90 minute talks on your book and business which will bring you many leads and a good amount of long term customers who will be very eager for your information.

Eventually, a connection will happen. Maybe it's the dad that is the CEO at a local company that needs a book written or it is the owner of a sporting goods shop that wants to sell your book on coaching basketball.

Even if the event never resulted in a professional contact, it has resulted in numerous personal ones. I've also spoken to small business groups about how to write a books to promote their businesses and then marketed them my information on that topic. There's a lot of opportunity right out your front door!

In addition to book signings, I recommend collaborating with associations and organizations.

For example, if you write a guidebook about how to breed

standard poodles, you can present material related to your subject at AKC meetings, the local humane society and rescue organizations.

As with book signings, the key to making a presentation effective, is to make it an event. Standing in front of a room and showing a slide show on point of sale is not going to be interesting for your potential customers. Instead, you can bring point of sale devices for demonstrations or case studies in video format.

One last consideration when you are speaking to promote your book, don't forget to bring copies of your book. Occasionally, associations will not want you to sell your book at the event. If this is the case, bring a copy for people to see and make order forms available, or offer a sign in sheet and ask for email addresses.

Once you return home, you can send an email to the attendees and pitch your book in the email.

I have a friend who often host workshops for small business organizations on how to create a marketing newsletter to increase sales. She does not bring a copy of her book on newsletter creation to the workshop. However, she will bring a copy of the free workbook that is include with her book. She also prints discount coupons for attendees if they are interested in purchasing her book after the workshop. Additionally, she collects business cards and document on the back of the card if the person has expressed interest in receiving more information.

Press releases are a very inexpensive way to get the word out about your book. You can send your release to media contacts and post it on the web. This makes it available to resources all over the world to reprint. My favorite is http://www.prweb.com/ and it offers helpful information on writing a press release that will get your book the attention that you want.

Planning a Press Release

The necessary preparation for a press release is much like any other type of business correspondence. A proper outline or writing plan will give you a good idea as to how you wish to approach the topic of your press release and the best way for you to convey your message in such a way that the media will find it newsworthy. After all, a press release is nothing if it's not worthy of being reported as news.

When planning your press release, make sure that you are constructing something that is new, different, exciting and interesting. These are all good characteristics of a press release and will attract various forms of media. Did you know that you can send a press release to both print and broadcast media? You can! Newspaper and magazine editors may choose to publish a story based solely on your press release, but will most likely reword the content for editorial and space restrictions. A television or radio station, however, will use your press release differently in that you may be invited to participate in a live, on-air interview. In this instance, the subject of your press release will likely be discussed, along with other aspects of your project.

Defining your target audience will help you to structure the press release in a way that will make your news appealing. As an author, your main purpose will be to inform the readers of your new book. As someone in search of media attention, however, your overall purpose will be to entice the media to report your project as news. This will give both you and your book credibility, but will also increase your visibility to the public and create the potential for new customers.

Before getting started on your press release, make sure that you gather all of your information and take the time to look it over one final time. You should also have a single paragraph reserved at the conclusion of your press release, which will feature your website address (if applicable), professional background and/or company history.

CREATING YOUR PRESS RELEASE

A press release is an official statement issued to the media, which entices them to report your news to the public. In order for your news to actually make the news, you have to know how to create a press release that will convince the media to run your story. A good press release will be the difference between free publicity and no publicity, which is why its creation is essential in promoting your new book.

As an author, your press release will obviously be focusing on your new book. This means that you should include a brief summary of the book, a paragraph highlighting your education and professional experience, the publication date, price, ISBN and the publisher's name in the context of your press release. The majority of media outlets also require that the individual who submits the press release (that's you!) must include their name, address and telephone number beneath the heading of the press release. In addition to giving the editor a way to contact you and verify the information, it also gives them the opportunity to get in touch and schedule an interview.

Okay, so now you have the essentials. You know what facts to incorporate, but you still need an intro that will grab the attention of your readers. After all, the first person to read your press release will be an editor. If the first few lines in your text doesn't capture their attention, you may not have a lot of luck in getting it published. But don't worry; I'm about to tell you how to get the hook that you need to make your press release sizzle.

Title your press release with a headline that grabs the reader by the eyeballs and makes them want to read more. For instance, let's say you are a realtor that has just written the book on how to sell your house for more money.

A good headline might be:

"New Book Shows Property Owners How To Make An Extra $25,000.00 From The Sale Of Their House With Little Known $20.00 Home Accessory"

A poor headline might be:

"Learn Some New Ideas For Selling Your House"

The first headline says "I have to find out how to make an extra $25,000.00," the second headline elicits a "Who Cares?" response.

A headline that makes the reader want more information will always get you the response you want. You must hook them into your story enough that they will want more information. When you use a direct response headline like the one above your response rate will increase dramatically.

To learn how to write a good headline or title quickly just buy an Enquirer newspaper or a Cosmopolitan Magazine and look at their headlines. There is a reason why those publications do so well and you can do the same thing by getting ideas from the headlines they use.

Now that you have the perfect title, make sure that the first few lines of your press release are nothing short of spectacular. This is the point where editors and potential customers will decide whether or not your news is worth reading. Lets say that you are continuing with the same theme of a how to make more money selling your house as previously noted. The first few lines of your press release could read:

"It's Amazing. A new book, written by John Doe who has been in the real estate business for 25 years, highlights an important home selling device. Doe discovered an important little home accessory that always seemed to make a home sell for more money. At first he did not know why these particular homes sold for more but then one day figured it out while sitting in the customer's kitchen. Anyone can use this to make more money selling their homes."

I think you see my point. Your first few sentences have to

reach out and grab the reader. It has to pull them into the story and make them not want to look away. If they even think about looking away, you want them to be too curious to stop reading.

How To Properly Format A Press Release

Print media people can be picky about the format of press release you send them. Sometimes if you don't do it their way, you will raise a big red flag that you are an amateur. Other types of media outlets aren't as fussy, but you might as well learn the "correct way" for print media and then make all your press releases the same.

Your press releases must:

- Be on your letterhead.
- Be no more than 500 words or one page in length.
- Have 1 inch to 1.25 inch margins all around
- Be double spaced.
- Include the date of the release in the first paragraph.
- Have a quick, two to three sentence compelling summary paragraph before the press release begins.
- Include your contact information – name and phone number – in the upper right corner above the headline. You must be available for contact by the media. They don't like leaving messages and they usually don't call back.
- Title your release with a headline that makes the recipient want to read more

Sample Press Release:

FOR IMMEDIATE RELEASE

Contact:
John Doe

BreakthroughBball.Net
Phone: 319-555-1212
Fax: 1-309-555-1212
Email: John@breakthroughbball.net
http://www.breakthroughbball.net

Designed To Ease Coaching Struggles, Unique New Book Offers Coaches Motivational Tips and 70 Free, Full Color Basketball Drills.

Announcing a unique new book, Winning BBall Drills, designed to addresses coaching struggles to motivate players by providing coaches motivational tips inside their free and well organized guide. This full color book also includes drill variations and step-by-step instructions for 70 fun and effective drills.

Marion, Iowa, November 15, 2006 -- Basketball coaches around the world struggle to keep their players motivated to improve their skills. "Winning BBall Drills," available for a free download at http://www.BBall.net, addresses this struggle by providing an easy and organized collection of drills, tips, and drill variations that not only help coaches motivate their players, they'll see players' skills improve.

Author, John Doe, has more than 30 years experience playing and coaching basketball teams at various levels. He understands both the struggles of motivating players, and what it takes to keep a player interested in improving their skills. His passion for basketball and his understanding of the needs of both coaches and players motivated him to write this free book.

The **Winning BBall Drills** book covers the following drill categories:

- Shooting Drills
- Passing Drills
- Ball Handling / Dribbling Drills
- Offense / Footwork Drills
- Big Man / Post Play Drills
- Transition Drills

- Defensive & Agility Drills
- Rebounding Drills

Website visitors are also offered an opportunity to sign up for their free monthly email newsletter, Bball Coaching Tips. Each newsletter offers coaches new basketball drills, proven end of game basketball plays, scoring tips, conditioning secrets, motivation tips, tips on how to improve defense, tips on how to lower turnovers, and helpful articles about running an effective program.

"Coaching basketball is a lot like running a business," says owner John Doe. John owns and successfully operates three businesses and has been a manager and business owner for more than 15 years. "As a coach, you have to manage projects, time, people, statistics, processes, and all kinds of things -- much like a business."

"I've discovered that the business fundamentals I have studied and learned over the years, greatly help me as a basketball coach. It is our hope that basketball coaches everywhere can take this knowledge and build successful, winning teams."

The information provided in Breakthrough BBall and Winning BBall Drills helps coaches organize and run their team efficiently to maximize their strengths and negate their weaknesses.

For additional information visit http://www.bballdrills.net or http://www.breakthroughbball.net or contact John at 319-555-1212.

BreakthroughBball.net was founded by basketball coach John Doe. His mission is to provide basketball coaches, players, and fans quality information about the sport that he loves.

-END-

PREPARING FOR MEDIA INTERVIEWS

Congratulations on having landed a media interview! You are

well on your way to literary stardom, If you let the interviewer know that you have a Q & A sheet for them they will love you because they know they are dealing with a pro. Of course this also make their life much easier and if you make it easy for them they will love you.

Following is an example of a Q & A I have used in the past and note that it also helps them with an introduction found at the bottom of the Q & A

CONTACT NUMBER - (604) 555-1234

**Suggested Questions for Bob Burnham,
Authority on Great Customer Services and Fire/
Flood Restoration Expert**

1. What does it mean to love your customers?

2. Why is your customer service method so successful?

3. There are a lot of painters and carpet cleaners in the market why do people prefer to deal with your company?

4. Exactly where do most service companies go wrong?

5. You've been quoted as saying: "If you can't make it in the customer service business, it's your own fault." That seems pretty harsh! What do you mean by that?

6. What are your thoughts on unreasonable customers?

7. How do you feel about the service industries future?

8. How important is the first impression in the service business?

9. What help do you have for anyone that wants to get into the service business?

10. Who has more success in the service industry, men or women?

11. Does age have any bearing on the success people have in the service business?

12. How important is training?

Why do people need to train in customer service? Shouldn't all this come naturally?

13. What 3 things can service company's do today to increase their business right away?

14. What's your favorite customer service story?

15. Why is it so important to love your customers?

16. How can people get in touch with you? (They can call 1-800-555-1234)

Suggested Introduction for Bob Burnham

Bob Burnham an IICRC Certified Master Restoration Technician and is the owner of several fire and flood restoration companies. He is currently building a chain of Painting, Carpet Cleaning and Home Repair service companies under the BurnMac Services brand name. He is an authority on good customer service and can tell you how to avoid the mistakes that can cause customers to go to your competition. Be sure to have a pen and paper handy. He'll be giving you information you won't want to miss.

Here's one last but very important way to promote your self-published book...

Chapter 6

Take It To The Races

A Step-By-Step Guide To Setting Up A Website For Maximum Book Sales

Selling Your Book On A Website-a Step By Step Guide To Setting Up And Promoting Your Website For Maximum Book Sales

If you already have a website that people visit, and you've written on a topic that is relevant to your career/products/or services, you can add a bookstore page to your website. By listing your book on your website, you're showing visitors right then and there that you're the expert! And it's easy to link your book directly to Amazon, (even more credibility). All your visitor needs to do is click on your book and they're taken directly to Amazon to make a purchase.

If you don't have a website, you may want to get one. It's very easy to direct people to your website for a purchase and if you decide to add more products to your funnel: workbooks, audio books, speaking engagements, consulting, etc, then you'll definitely want a single source of information for your potential customers!

First Step... a Domain Name

One of the best ways to sell your book is to sell it yourself on your own website. This accomplishes many things.

The first step to getting a website is to choose a domain name. Your domain name is the URL that people will type into their browser to get to your site.
Example: http://www.bestsellingbooks.com Your domain name is bestesllingbooks.com.

There are thousands of places to register your domain name, too many to mention. I suggest that you register your domain name at the same place that you have host your website because it's easier. It eliminates domain transfers and fees that arise from transfers.

Before you register your domain name, you need to choose a name. Then you will need to verify that your name choice is available.

Choosing a Domain Name

Name your domain after your book - Your book is called the How to Eat Away Arthritis so you call your website www. eatawayarthritis.com.

You can also name the website after yourself or your pen name.

If you're planning to add more books on the same subject, you might want to look for a domain name that is representative of the type of information that you'll be providing.

For example, if you're offering a book on training dogs, then you might want your site to be called www. bestdogtraining.com. If you are able to get one or two of your main keywords into your URL this can help down the road with some free organic traffic.

Once you have an idea of what you want to call your website, you can visit just about any domain name registration site and find out if your domain name is available by using their domain name search tool. It's free.

Choosing a Website Host

Finding a website host can be an overwhelming task. There are hundreds of thousands of web hosting companies. Fortunately, there are websites that allow you to compare some hosting companies against each other using information like price, features, capacity, and more.

Here's what you need to know:

1. Your hosting company should have a solid reputation and longevity in the industry. If they're a minor operation, you run the risk of your website going down, not having the IT support that you need when you need it, and the business going under leaving you high and dry.

2. Your hosting company should have a competitive price, but do not always go for the cheapest!

3. Your hosting company should have the features that you want/need. For example, if you're considering blogging, newsletters, auto responders, shopping cart software, then many hosting companies offer all of these features with a business website package.

Choose three to four hosting plans to compare and then look for reviews on your chosen hosting plans. Speak with others to find out if they're happy with their service provider.

1. Make sure that your hosting plan is easy for you to use. Some of us, me included, are not technologically inclined. Some hosts offer customizable website templates. (This isn't always the best idea because you want to differentiate your website from others, but it can be helpful.)

2. If on the other hand, you're going to do your website yourself via FrontPage, Dreamweaver, or other website developing software, then you'll need to make sure that your hosting company offers you the ability to upload your web pages.

Once you've decided on a hosting company and registered your domain name, you're ready to design your website! Remember that you can hire people to handle some of these tasks for you. Website design is definitely one of those areas that you may want to outsource.

I have attempted to design my own websites numerous times and it always ends up in frustration and hours of wasted time. Eventually, I admitted defeat and hired a professional.

If, on the other hand, you're a do-it-yourselfer, then the next section will give you what you need to know to get started....

WEBSITE DESIGN 101

BE A GOOD CONTRACTOR

Whether you decide to do all or part of your website yourself you will still ultimately be subcontracting parts of the process. Just like building a house it is important for you to be a good contractor. You must be clear in your communication in instructing and hiring for you to get the best website for your money.

Designing your website is fun for some and a headache for others.

If you'd rather not do it all by yourself, you can:

- Use a template
- Hire a website designer
- Freelance websites like Elance.com
- Yellow Pages or local search engines

- Alternatively, you can hire technologically inclined students!
- Hire someone to design parts of your website.

If you want to do it yourself, it can be a very easy thing to do and you can do parts of it yourself and leave other parts for the experts.

For example, if you want to develop the basic layout yourself but you don't want to handle the design of the graphics, like a logo or banner for the top of your website, you can hire a designer.

If you want to get ideas for the layout and design for your website, visit websites of other authors and your competitors and see what you like and don't like about their sites.

If you see a website that you'd like to emulate, click on the view button in your browser toolbar and view the source code for the site. Website design isn't copyrighted so you're fee to use any template/design that you'd like. What is copyrighted often is the copy and potentially the images that you see. There are a variety of image banks online that you can visit to find appropriate graphics for your website including

- Big Stock photo
- Photo Search
- I Stock Photo
- Shutter Stock
- Big Photo

And much more. There is a fee for using the images and you need to make sure that you're purchasing unlimited rights so that you can use the image in any medium you'd like. This means that you'll be able to develop a consistent look between your website and some of your print materials; brochures, letterhead etc,

Using the viewed website as a template, you can then copy the page and paste it into your website builder software or into any basic html tool.

You can then play around with changing the site to fit your design and copy needs. It is almost like using a template.

You can also find templates available for free or for purchase online. Many websites provide these, including:

- http://www.templatemonster.com/
- http://www.templatesbox.com/

The great thing about marketing a book is that the website requirements are minimal. You really only need a one or two-page website. The first page, your landing page, will be the sales copy. Your second page is your order form, if you're selling it yourself. If you're linking to a bookstore, then you don't even need a second page.

You can of course have more pages in your site, but a general rule of thumb is to include everything on your landing page that you need to sell the book.

Why? Because, you don't want your website visitors to have to click through for more information. Every chance you give them to click is a decision that your visitors have to make, and every decision they have to make is another chance for a decision to leave your website. Your website must be easy to navigate because a confused mind does not buy.

How To Write Winning Web Copy to Sell Your Book.

There are actually two main types of sales copy that work well for converting browsers into book buyers.

The first type of landing page has a more editorial feel to it. You'd still offer a headline that attracts attention but the copy will appear more like an article than a sales letter. I like this kind of copy because it doesn't have the look or feel of a typical sales letter, which can turn off visitors simply looking for information and not a sales pitch.

This type of sales copy still points out the problem to be solved but also details in an article style how to solve the problem and then it goes into how there's more to know and how your book can help.

The other style of landing page is the long copy sales letter. The numbers don't lie, long copy sells. And the formula for how much copy you should write is as follows: As much copy as you need to convince your prospect to purchase your book.

Must Haves for Winning Sales Copy

1. An attention grabbing headline
2. Identify a problem and then agitate it, show your reader's why it the problem is worse than they think..
3. Offer a solution to the customer's problem. Include an emotional statement about the problem and offer a solution -- your book.
4. Stress benefits (not features)
5. Differentiate yourself from your competitors
6. Provide proof: testimonials, case studies, facts, comparisons, etc.
7. Establish credibility: testimonials, client list, for example: as seen on ABC, CBS, or MTV.
8. Build value (offer bonuses...you can easily compile a list of resources, offer free reports either written by yourself or someone else, offer worksheets, tip sheets, etc.)
9. Don't forget your call to action. BUY NOW!
10. A sense of urgency. Act now because the book is only available at this price for the first 30 buyers.
11. Don't forget to use emotion and active words!

Include in your sales letter the above key features and you're good to go.

In addition to your website design and copy, you will need to integrate keywords and keyword phrases into your copy and your code. This will enable the search engines to list you in their results.

Here's how to do it...

SEARCH ENGINE OPTIMIZATION

Natural search listings are search engine results that are not paid for. They're also known as organic search results. By improving your natural search results, you move up on the rankings and increase your visibility to potential customers. As your search engine ranking improves, so does your store traffic.

Step #1 Keyword Research

Keywords are the words that your customers would type into the search engine to find you and your book, for example "Cat Tricks." More important than keywords are keyword phrases, for example "Impossible Cat Training," "Funny Cat Tricks," or "Potty Training Your Cat."

The creation of appropriate and relevant keyword phrases reduces the amount of key word competition you'll have when potential customers are searching.

Tip: Develop appropriate keyword phrases for your site

1. One method to develop keyword phrases for your website is to brainstorm with friends and family to come up with relevant and appropriate keyword phrases for your site. Consider what potential customers might search for and write it down. Just let your imagination fly!

2. The second method to develop keywords and keyword phrases is to utilize keyword tools like Wordtracker or the Google Keyword Tool that we discussed earlier.

Step #2 Optimize Your Website

Search engines look at the structure and coding of your website. For this reason, it is important to place your key words where the search engines look. You should also optimize each important page of your website for two or three different keyword phrases.

Note that if you use too many keyword phrases, you run the risk of decreasing the quality of your content.

PLACE YOUR KEYWORDS IN YOUR TITLE TAG

Your HTML code includes a title tag. The title tag is essentially the HTML code that creates the words that appear in the top bar of your Web browser and one of the first "structural elements" of a website that a search engine will look for.

If your main keyword is "Book Publishing," the HTML code for your title tag might look like this:

```
<head>
<title>Step-By-Step Guide to Book
Publishing</title>
</head>
```

Add Your Keywords Phrases to the Heading Tags (<H1>)

Search engines actively seek out the headings in your content. These headings are identified by search engines with the <H1> tag.

The heading tags give the search engines something to focus on and they tell them what your page is about.

Many of the engines place considerable weight on heading tags.

You'll want to put some consideration into your headings and the keywords that you want to use.

<H1>The Most Comprehensive Information On Training Dogs</H1>

Your keywords in your heading are "Training Dogs" Make sure that the copy you provide under your headings includes information that relates to the heading, and it provides your reader with information.

Use Your Keywords in Your Sales Letter/Landing Page

As you construct your sales copy, use your keyword phrases both in the headings and in the body copy. Don't go overboard and use too many keywords. Instead, choose two or three and focus on using the words efficiently and effectively.

We'll get more into keyword placement and how to craft your copy in the next section, but first I want to talk briefly about shopping cart software because if you're selling the book yourself, you'll need a means to collect money and provide customer's receipts.

Shopping Cart Software Choices

- If your web hosting company doesn't offer shopping cart software, or you prefer to use a different option, consider shopping cart software like 1shoppingcart that offers newsletters, auto responders, and more to make the entire process automated and easy for you and your customer.

- Another popular option for selling your book online is ClickBank. ClickBank is a web company/service that handles the shopping cart aspect of your sales. You're still responsible for the website and for fulfillment but for an initial fee and a percentage of each sale, they'll take care of the ordering process.

- Link to a major bookseller like amazon.com or barnesandnoble.com to handle the sales of your self-published book.

- There are also ecommerce templates that you can purchase on the web and upload into your web design.

- In addition, there are stores that you can establish via Yahoo, PayPal, and more.

Look at these software and shopping cart software choices from the eyes of your customer. Seek shopping cart software that gives your customers confidence in you and your book, makes the transaction easy for them, and is trustworthy, safe, and secure.

Type "shopping cart software comparison" into your search engine of preference and review the options. The following is a site that gives a good overview of many shopping cart products: http://shopping-cart-review.toptenreviews.com/

Remember that you can start small and test a product. If it doesn't work out, the only thing you've lost is a little time.

Life is what you make it.

– Origin Unknown

Chapter 7

Traffic?! Promoting Your Book's Website For More Sales

PROMOTING YOUR BOOK'S WEBSITE

I've talked a bit on how to name and design your website. I've also discussed shopping cart and pricing decisions. What I have yet to discuss is the meat of any book marketer's book selling campaign -- promoting your website.

The key to successful book sales is a successful website. To be successful, a website will need to be viewed by a large number of people. It also needs to be able to convert those visitors into customers.

HOW TO DRAW WEBSITE VISITORS AND SELL BOOKS.

- **Search Engine Optimization.** It is important that your website is positioned well with the major search engines. More than 70% of internet users say that they use the internet for research. If you're not positioned on the search engines, then internet users will not be able to find you easily.

- Optimal search engine positioning will not happen overnight. However, with patience, persistence, and knowledge you can earn top rankings. There are several steps to take and tools to use to position your website with the search engines.

- **Irresistible sales copy.** If you want to turn website visitors into customers, then convincing sales copy is a must. Fortunately, once you know the secrets of crafting winning sales copy, your work is done. One effective sales letter can be used for decades without needing any changes! Effective sales copy utilizes many secrets, secrets like powerful headlines, emotional appeals, stressing benefits over features, using testimonials and reviews, and much more.

- **An Opt-in list.** An opt-in list is a book marketer's direct line to current and potential customers. Opt in lists are generally built by offering website visitors free information in exchange for their email address or by asking them to subscribe to a newsletter. Regular communication with an opt-in list is proven to build book sales.

- **A Squeeze Page.** You can have a separate page you send readers to from your signature at the end of an article. This page would be set up where you require their name and email address for free downloadable information like a chapter of your book, a report, or even a downloadable audio file.

- The conversation rates (Customers who opt-in) can be from 20% and even as high as 65%. The opt-in % is usually lower if you just have an opt-in box on your web page. The key here is to test to determine what will work best for you.

- **Autoresponders.** Autoresponders are one of the
  tools that you will use to communicate with your
  opt-in list. Autoresponders are automated, scheduled
  emails, sent to your opt-in list and to your customers.
  Autoresponders can be a simple paragraph announcing
  a new promotion, or they can be a detailed article
  designed to educate and sell to your customer.

They are the perfect tool because they can be written in
advance and then set up to be sent automatically, at defined
intervals, to clients that purchase your book or to prospects that
trade their email address for free information.

Auto responders are usually designed as a group of
messages. If a person has signed up to receive your newsletter,
then you can send them a series of short sales messages two or
three days apart.

If a person has made a book purchase, you can send an
auto responder message to them a day later letting them know
that you appreciate their purchase. You can then let them know
about future books or other information that you have available
on your website. You can send a message a week later asking for
feedback on your book, which you can then use as a testimonial.

Like all your sales copy and your book, the language of
your auto responder should be friendly and informal.

The trick to making auto responders and all email
campaigns easy to track, manage, and set up is finding a
software program that works for you. Another great use for an
auto responder is for your regular newsletter mailing.

The auto responder I use is AWeber because they are
reliable and have a very good delivery rate. Go to: http://www.
aweber.com/?214107

How Newsletters Increase Your Website Traffic and Your Customer's Lifetime Value

Let's look at two of the most important benefits of a

newsletter. The benefits are increasing your website traffic and increasing your customer's lifetime value.

Newsletters increase traffic when:

- **Content is forwarded.** Despite the abundance of newsletters available, not all content is quality and not all content is relevant to everyone. However, through persistence and regular email campaigns, relevant content will be noticed and potentially forwarded to friends, family, and associates (assuming you haven't forgotten the forward to a friend option in your newsletter) resulting in an increase in website traffic and the potential to gain new prospects.

- **Search engine searches lead to newsletter archives.** 70% of US households use the Internet to search for information before they make a purchase. Imagine if your newsletter articles, archived on your website, show up on the search engines, resulting in a click-through to your website and a potential new customer.

- **New leads and prospects are gained.** Email addresses are acquired when subscribing, allowing you to generate email campaigns targeted to specific lists

- **Content is valuable.** Again, valuable content is appreciated and consistent newsletters filled with valuable content can position you and your company as leaders in the industry and a resource for solving your prospects' needs when they arise.

- **Content is regular.** Newsletters are by definition regular installments of information. By entering your prospect's mailbox on a regular basis, you stay foremost in their minds and are more likely to be there when your prospect is ready to make a purchase.

Customer lifetime value is a marketing tool that projects the value of a customer over the entire history of that customer's relationship with a company. Email newsletters increase your customer's lifetime value because they are not only inexpensive marketing tools, but they help you keep the customers that you have. Email newsletters can breed familiarity, loyalty, and they can make purchasing easy.

While also being a measurable marketing tool, email newsletters also offer many benefits. They have a very high response rate. They provide increased brand awareness. Additionally, they are a valuable marketing tool for any bookseller. In short, they're a winning solution to increasing website traffic and customer lifetime value.

- **Valuable Content.** Content plays two roles on your website. When you utilize search engine optimization strategies within your information content is used to draw visitors to your website. Press releases and published articles will also draw visitors to your website.

Additionally, quality content provided to website visitors will keep visitors returning to your website and making purchases. This content can be provided to your visitors by placing it directly on your website or by emailing it as a newsletter or auto responder.

There are several important steps to creating quality content on your website. The content must be informative. The content must be relevant. The content should also be entertaining and hopefully it also promotes your book.

The last thing that you should consider when promoting your book on your website is generating a marketing plan.

Your marketing plan can be as simple as writing the dates that you will release articles, announce promotions, distribute press releases and deliver your newsletter. Don't forget that you do not have to handle all of this yourself. Marketing specialists, public relations representatives, and administrative assistants can be extremely helpful.

LIST BUILDING—THE KEY TO MORE BOOK SALES

You have your website up and running and you have your book perfectly placed. You know your target market and you're eager to go. Now what? How do you get people to visit your website? How do you let them know what you have to offer? Better yet, once they know you're out there, how do you stay fresh in their minds?

A primary method is through an "opt-in list," your collection of email addresses from people who have expressed interest in your book. Without an opt-in list, your book may not reach enough ears and eyes to make it profitable.

Your list should include:
- People you know personally
- People you have corresponded with
- People that have expressed an interest in your book

You can add to your list by drawing people to your website with promotional vehicles. Utilize the marketing tools that we've discussed like blogs, articles, newsletters, free reports, and special offers. Once a potential customer is at your website, ask them to exchange their contact information or email address for a free chapter. Now you have a contact.

INCREASE YOUR WEBSITE TRAFFIC WITH A CONTENT RICH WEBSITE

You can also draw customers to your website by making it content rich. By this, I mean that you should keep the tone of the content informative. The Internet is full of people trying to sell things, yet as consumers we are primarily looking for information. Visitors are much more likely to spend time at your site if you're providing them with valuable content and not blatantly selling to them. They're also much more likely to trust you with their contact information.

Not sure how to make your content more informative?

Reprint articles on your website that you have published, either on the web or in print. Reprint interviews that you have conducted or workshops that you've run. You can even reprint speeches that you've given. It's all good, relevant content.

Also, consider adding information on topics related to your industry.

The possibilities for content ideas are endless. It is important to make sure that your site provides enough valuable content that people not only want to spend time there, but they also want to return. Your website should provide enough content that your visitors want to subscribe to your opt-in list or newsletter.

Lastly, I think it is important to address how frequently you contact your list. There are some website owners that email each day and others that only send out email once per month, There is no general rule on how often you should email but I will say that frequency builds familiarity. I think another good point to consider is that the fortune is in the follow up.

Keep a close watch and see how your customers are responding to the frequency of your emails. Always be testing for the best results. You can send a calendar of book signing dates, scheduled talks, and any sales or book promotions to keep your customers informed.

Building a solid list takes time and patience. However, it can be well worth the effort. These quality contacts may not only become future customers, word of mouth and email forwarding can lead you to additional customers. Treat your opt-in list with the same respect and consideration that you expect from others and you'll reap the rewards.

There are of course several paid ways that you can draw people to your website including:

- Affiliate Marketing
- Pay Per Click
- Adwords
- Banner Ads

- Paid links

And much more. The bottom line is that once your book is self published, there are tons of ways to attract attention to your website and your book. Don't dive in and use them all at once. First try the method that works for you, feels the most comfortable, and fits your needs. If it isn't as successful as you'd like it to be, then you can try another tool. On the other hand, if it works like gangbusters, then run with it!

Your ultimate goal of course is to become number one on Amazon's BestSellers list. Here's how to do it:

The most important thing you can do on Amazon is create an effective listing. For this you'll need a detailed description of your book. This should be very well written, take a look at your sales letter and the copy on the back of your book for guidance. What will your reader gain by reading your book? What are the specific benefits they'll receive? Use this formula:

You will discover:

1

2

3

4

etc...

Close the sale with a call for action. For example, "This book has made it possible for millions of people to self publish and achieve their personal and financial goals and it will show you the way too!"

You'll also want your bio as the author. This should include any information about you that will help to establish your credibility on the subject and an expert in your field.

Your book's listing will also include your front and back cover. You can add more images from the inside of your book if you think they are good selling points, and I highly recommend that you add your table of contents. You can also add a sample chapter, excerpts, and even a message from the author. All of these listing elements will help your book sell.

CATEGORIZE YOUR BOOK CORRECTLY

Many people search Amazon with a specific subject in mind.
Make sure that you categorize your book correctly and that you
create a listing that describes your book accurately using search
keywords, your name, and even your book's title. People will
browse Amazon in a variety of ways, by your name, by your
book's title, and by your subject matter. Make sure all of these
are addressed in your listing.

REVIEWS

Some people rely quite heavily on reviews when making their
buying decision. A handful of really great book reviews can
be just the thing you need to send your book to the top of the
bestseller's list.

So…as soon as your listing appears on Amazon, or Barnes
and Noble, ask friends, business associates and anyone you can
think of that has read your book to post a favorable review. You
can also ask anyone from your email list that has bought your
book to write a review. Good reviews will help to sell your book.

UTILIZE PROMOTIONAL OPPORTUNITIES WITH AMAZON AND BARNES & NOBLE.

Both major online booksellers enable you to utilize a variety of
tools to promote your book. They include:

Amazon Connect. An email service that enables you to
connect with your readers.

Author Profile Pages. This enables you to create a web page
to promote your book, yourself, post a message, and link to our
personal website. Best of all…it's free!

Amazon Associate. This is more of an affiliate program
where you can create your own online bookstore and earn a
commission from selling other people's books and products,

however you can use this to sell your own books and products too.

Barnes & Noble Meet The Writers. Is an author profile feature. If you want to be featured here, send information about yourself, your book and your contact info to writers@book.com

Become An Amazon Best Seller Coaching and Mentoring

When in doubt, contact the experts. There are a number of coaches and mentors that specialize in helping you get your book on the best seller list.

There is even one website that guarantees that you will be an Amazon Best Seller. This in my view is worth either the money to have them do it or the effort to do it yourself by following their formula. You will be impressed with some of the books they have been a part of for becoming a best seller on Amazon.

The headline on their site is:

We'll Help You Make Your
Book An Amazon.com Bestseller
in Just 38 Days … Guaranteed!

Your life will really change once you say you are a best selling author and it can be done

Go To: http://www.bestsellermentoring.com

There is also a second mentor that is very good at what he does named Warren Whitlock at:

http://marketingresultscoach.com

Using a coach or mentor will help you by:

*Eliminating any first timer mistakes that beginners often make.

*Help you from the very beginning to meet your financial and career goals. They'll guide you and let you know if your book idea is on the right track.

*Can help you go from self-published to a big time publishing contract with a major publishing house. Remember, if they come to you then you have more control to negotiate your contract!

The only downside to hiring a coach is that you'll have to spend some money. However, when you do become a Best Seller on Amazon, then your return on investment will be tenfold and I am probably being a bit conservative when I say that.

The following are some mentors/coaches that specialize in helping self publishers attain their goals:

http://www.writershelper.com/mentor.html

http://www.parapublishing.com

If you can dream it, you can do it.

– *Walt Disney*

Chapter 8

Hitting the Highway

How To Make More Money Than You Ever Imagined!

Your book is done. It's published. You've listed it on Amazon. You've established a website and you're all ready to make tons of money, expand your horizons and opportunities, and reach the goals that you have established for your life.

Your work is done, right?

Not quite.

Are you really going to stop here? Are you going to let tens of thousands, hundreds of thousands, of dollars pass you by?

No, I didn't think so.

Your book is only the top of a very lucrative iceberg. Your very own information marketing empire! This is the fork in the road that separates the Unsuccessful and Broke Authors from the Successful and Rich Authors.

You see there is a big difference between Unsuccessful and Broke Authors and Successful and Rich Authors and that is:

Unsuccessful and Broke Authors think they are in the writing business.

Successful and Rich Authors know that they are in the marketing business.

Unsuccessful and Broke Authors think they will make money from royalties

Successful and Rich Authors make money from repackaging their book information and selling it as seminars, home study courses, CD's, coaching and consulting and many other products because they know that the book is just the start like a business card.

Broke authors can make money from royalties but the chances of getting rich are almost the same chances as winning a lottery. Rich authors know you can become rich from selling your information in different formats beginning with your book. Let me explain some of the different ways you can make money with your book through information marketing

WHAT IS INFORMATION MARKETING?

Information marketing is the packaging of information—your information—in a variety of mediums like reports, seminars, software, audio, video, and consulting.

For example, if you wrote a book on dog training you can easily sell it as an audio CD set or in an electronic downloadable eBook format. Instantly you have two more products to add to your website and product line.

The physical book may be $19.95 where as the CD version set might be $97.00 The profit margins on repackaging your information can be very good. In fact in the case of your 6 CD set your costs may only be $10.00 leaving almost $90.00 for pure profit. You have to sell a lot of books to make the same amount of profit as the CD set.

Another product may be to add a step-by-step training video of your information. This video set may be priced $197.00 and they are easy to make. The nice thing about this is you can sell the information over and over again without doing all the work over again.

If you are a dog trainer you just have to video tape the

lessons you would be teaching your students and then you can sell it over and over again.

How about a training seminar or workshop? What about a dog training audio or video series? The series could include potty training, teaching sit and stay, agility training, and even a tangent series on preparing raw dog food and optimal nutrition for your dog. The possibilities are endless. What about one on one coaching or an interactive CD Rom?

Why Build an Information Marketing Empire?

1. People learn differently. Some learn by watching and others learn by hearing or actually going through the motions. When you provide your information in a variety of mediums, you're respecting these learning styles and you're broadening your customer base and you're broadening your audience appeal.

2. People are more likely to buy from you again and again, if they liked their previous purchase and received benefit from it. This is why it is important to provide only quality products.

3. As you increase your product line, you can offer a variety of cost levels. For example, if your book costs $30 that is a great entry level price but some people may be interested in spending more to receive more. This is when offering a seminar or consulting services can meet the needs of the customers with the larger budget. By offering a variety of price points, you're broadening your target market.

4. More products gives people the perception that you are more than the expert in your field, you are the guru. You are the single best person to go to because you offer so many products in your niche field.

5. Not everyone will want to, or be able to, spend $3000 but if you present a product line, you have presented

them with numerous alternatives. It's like going to a bike store that only sells $7000 bikes or a bike store that only sells $300 bikes. These stores have a limited product line and will thus have a limited clientele. Customers only searching for really expensive or cheap bikes.

On the contrary, a bike store that sells bikes ranging in price from $300 to $7000 will have a much broader clientele. This is the way that your information product line will work too. If you only sell a book for $30 or you only sell consulting services for $3000 you will have a significantly limited clientele. But if you offer a variety of price points and products your clientele will have more options and you'll have a larger group of paying customers.

WHAT EVERY BOOKSELLER AND INFORMATION MARKETER MUST HAVE.

The number one thing that you must have, absolutely must have, is an opt-in list. A list of email addresses of people that have visited your website and/or are interested in your information.

We discussed an opt-in list earlier in the chapter on developing and promoting your website so I won't repeat myself. Just know that it is imperative that you capture every website visitor's email address.

How do you convince visitors to give you their email address? By giving away something for free.

You must give away something of value that will make them want to give you their name and email address. You can give away a special report or a 2 hour MP3. You can give away a chapter of your book. You can give away some one else's book. It doesn't really matter what you give away, but it has to be of quality and value. If you give them a quality free product, they'll know that the stuff you charge for is going to be outstanding!

The easiest way to collect email addresses from website visitors is to include a sign up form on your webpage. Don't ask for more than a name and email address because you won't get it. Statistics show that signup forms that ask for more information than an email address are ignored more often.

People don't trust you enough yet to give you too much information about themselves. Trade a product for their email address, provide a quality product, and you'll earn their trust and their business. Besides if you need more information from them, you can ask at a later date.

Why do you need their email address?

Simple, it is the number one best way to reach your prospective audience. It is virtually free and your message is instantaneous. AND with autoresponders working for you, emailing 1000's of people can take as little as a few minutes and the click of a button. Additionally, you can program a series of messages to go out to your prospects every other day, week or even once a month. Autoresponders are a fantastic tool and they'll make your life as an information marketer significantly easier.

Remember, when using autoresponders, these are your past, present, and future customers! There really is no hard and fast rule on how often you can send out an email but remember frequency breeds familiarity. The fortune is in the follow up so test your list to see how often they appreciate hearing from you.

TOOLS TO DRIVE TRAFFIC TO YOUR WEBSITE

I know, I know, I already talked about this. I just want to remind you what they are because they're important. If people aren't visiting your website, then they're not buying your book. Sure you have it listed on Amazon and of course you are telling everyone you know about your book but you could be reaching so many more people!

Don't forget:

Search Engine Optimization. Make sure you're being listed with the major search engines. Incorporate key words into your web content paying specific attention to the headlines and subheadings. Don't forget to submit your website to the search engines yourself or using your web hosts services to handle this task.

Pay Per Click is another tool to drive traffic to your website. This is a Google program where you bid on keywords that people might use to find the kind of information that you provide on your website. Try a few specific keywords and keyword phrases, don't go crazy and bid on tons of keywords. Test it. Make sure that it's driving traffic to your website before you invest too much money.

Last time I checked Google had about 8 hours of videos on how to use Adwords so take advantage of it. Also Perry Marshall has written a great book called 'Ultimate Guide to Google AdWords'.

Advertise on other websites and in e-zines with a relevant theme. You can find a list of e-zines at http://www.ezinedirectory.com

Co-registration is another tool to drive traffic to your website if you offer a newsletter or other list building device. Co-registration is where you partner with a company to advertise your newsletter along with similar newsletters. Every time someone subscribes to your newsletter, you pay the co-registration company a fee.

You can find many co-registration services by simply searching for the term on your favorite search engine. Two popular services are Co-regcomplete and Venture direct.

Another great way to drive traffic to your website is to have affiliate marketers. Affiliate marketers are people that sell your products for a commission. Many shopping cart programs that cater to the information marketing entrepreneur offer affiliate marketing support programs to help you facilitate the process, track and pay your affiliates.

One such shopping cart software is 1shoppingcart.com. They offer autoresponders, product delivery, electronic product delivery and affiliate marketing support.

How To Collect Email Addresses—Offline

How many people are in your rolodex right now? Add them to your information marketing email list. Hesitant? Place them in a separate group or email list and send them a separate email asking permission to add them to your list.

In addition to your current list, be on the lookout for every opportunity to add names to your list. If you attend a seminar, strike up conversations with the people around you. Find out what they do, what they're interested in and share your story. Chances are they, or someone that they know, will be interested in your information. Give them a business card with your web address on it, or better yet, collect their email address and send them a special note.

Remember when you go to a seminar in your niche market it is a good way to make new very targeted contacts and add them to your list. If you get good at talking about your information products to everyone you meet at a seminar you will find that most often you can make more money from the contacts and subsequent business that you actually paid for the seminar.

If you belong to an organization, association, or any type of group make sure that you place your website address on all documentation and directory. You never know where you're going to find your next best customer. Additionally, make sure that every article or press release that you publish has your website address on it.

You can consider yourself a walking talking opt-in box

by giving people your business card with a free gift offer on it so they will opt-in to your website. You could even have your Signature on the back of your card. Below is a sample of what you could put on the back of your card.

Bob Burnham, Entrepreneur, Consultant and Author of '101 Reasons Why You Must Write A Book'

For Your FREE MP3 (Value $97.00)

'How To Make A 6 Figure Income Writing & Publishing Your Own Book'

Go to: http://www.ExpertAuthorPublishing.com

If you speak at a seminar, make sure to pass around a signup list. One well known speaker actually uses the 'green sheet' method when he conducts seminars. It works like this: you hand out seminar materials and in the materials you include one piece of paper, maybe it's a slide from a power point presentation or maybe it's an ad for your next seminar.

You make that sheet green and you tell the audience that you have a book on the subject that you're talking about but that you didn't bring it. (Some times when you're hired to speak, you're asked to not sell your products directly.)

Anyway, you tell the audience that if they're interested in receiving a Free Report or book etc, what ever you decide you want to give that they can place their name on the "green sheet" and leave it at the front of the room. Now you've very discreetly acquired a whole room full of email addresses without making any kind of sales pitch.

So now that you know why you should sell information products, what are you going to sell?

CREATING A PRODUCT LINE.

Books. Your book must be your first product. Why? Because the public will perceive you as an expert if you have a book. If you don't...

You can have hundreds of information products but if

you don't have a book, it can be harder to sell other products. That's not to say that your book is going to be your biggest moneymaker. Probably not. In fact if your book is your biggest money maker you are leaving a fortune on the table by not selling other more profitable products. But your book is the proof that you are an expert. The other information products that are made from your book are where the big dollars are made.

Once you have your book completed, you easily have two more products for your product line—an e-book and an audio book. The content is there, you've already done the hard part. All you need to do now is produce the other versions.

Following is a list of Products you can sell and produce from your book. The list is only limited by your imagination:

1. Audio
2. Video
3. Newsletter
4. Special reports
5. Teleseminar
6. Coaching
7. Consulting
8. Seminars, Conference & Boot camps
9. Online courses
10. ECourse
11. Home Study Courses
12. Membership sites
13. Continuity programs
14. Meet and Greet Events
15. Licensing
16. Joint ventures
17. Field trips
18. Talk shows

19. Discussion groups
20. Critiques
21. Templates
22. Do it for them packages
23. Software

It is endless and is only limited by your imagination and it can all be information that starts and spins out from your book. Everyone has different ways they like to learn and you can make a huge amount of money serving all those different groups.

Special Reports. The next product that you should add to your product line is a special report or a series of special reports. A special report is nothing more than a very specific article. It doesn't have to be more than 5 pages, probably shouldn't be longer than 20.

Creating a series of reports can be lucrative. While an individual report won't cost much, if you also offer a boxed set or a buy five get one free kind of offer, then you're likely to sell more of them.

For example: Using the dog training book example consider all of the special reports that can be offered:

- 10 easy ways to recognize an angry dog.
- 10 easy ways to make your dog feel safe.

Or you could take it on a tangent health and care niche:

- 10 ways to treat arthritis in your dog.
- 10 ways to treat diabetes
- How to give your dog the best diet possible.

Etc...the options for reports are endless.

When you sell your special reports, the best way to sell them is electronically. Make them available as a downloadable PDF so that customers are able to receive the instant information that they crave.

You can also package the series in book format and sell it as an e-book or printed book.

Audio Products. We've already discussed presenting your book as an audio book but did you know that you can also record interviews, teleseminars, seminars, and workshops and sell them as audio products? Audio opens up an entirely new world of products for you and many customers prefer audio products.

Take care to invest the time and money to offer a quality audio product. You can purchase your own audio equipment or rent audio equipment, or even hire professionals to do it for you. Sell your audio products as MP3s or digital downloads or package them as CDs.

If you're able to offer a variety of options to your customers, then all the better. You might, however, want to offer your audio product in one format to begin and then if it is a super seller, offer it in a new format. For example if the CDs sell super well, then you can rest assured that a downloadable file will sell well too.

Video—Video, like audio, opens up an entire new opportunity to create products for your line. Video sells well and is on a rising trend. With today's technology not only is very easy to create it is also very inexpensive to create and produce.

Every time you have a class seminar or any type of event you should be video taping it because you will then have another product. You will be creating more and more product as you progress and then selling it an high profits for years to come.

You can even sell the videos to the people that have just spent a weekend at your seminar. Let the participants know that you will be selling the videos of the weekend seminar to the public but because they have taken the seminar for the weekend they will get it at a reduced rate from what others will pay.

You will find a lot of the seminar attendees will order the video so they can keep referring back to it. They already know how good the information is so they buy it and this of course raises your profits for your weekend seminar.

Computer Software. Most niche topics are compatible with computer software products. Dog training, for example, might not immediately come to mind when people think of software however there are actually a myriad of products that could be designed for the topic.

- What about a dog training scheduler?
- A health tracking software program to record veterinary visits and necessary health issues to look for as a dog ages.
- What about a dog scrap booking program?
- How about an interactive dog training product?

I'm just brainstorming here but there are a variety of software options for any industry and the good news is that developing a product doesn't have to cost much. Much like a ghostwriter, you can hire a coder, to do the work for you. Visit rentacoder.com or scriptlance.com to post your project and have professional coders bid on it. Remember the guidelines for choosing a ghostwriter and choose wisely.

SEMINARS, BOOT CAMPS AND WORKSHOPS.

Now we're working our way into the more lucrative products. Seminars can be a very significant boost to your income and not just from the ticket sales. Many attendees will purchase your products after they hear you speak. They'll not only become lifelong customers, they'll tell others and your empire will continue to grow.

Seminars can be held as frequently or infrequently as you like. If you're new to speaking, then I recommend starting locally. Begin by offering a seminar through your local chamber of commerce or continuing education center. Your first few seminars can be offered at a lower ticket cost until you get your shtick down and are comfortable with your material and comfortable presenting.

If you're a seasoned speaker, then you're ahead of the game! Jump right in and begin earning those profits!

Teleseminars. In addition to hosting a seminar in person, teleseminars are a fantastic way to reach a large number of people that just can't travel to hear you speak. Additionally, teleseminars cost less because you don't have to rent a facility.

Many people host teleseminars for free and use them as a marketing tool to sell their products. Of course, whether you charge for your teleseminar or not, you should absolutely record the event and sell it as a product in your product line.

Online Courses. Does your niche topic appeal to others as an online course? Many topics do. From catering to software development, web design, dog training, and even gardening can all be taught online.

Fortunately, there are websites that make it easy to host an online course. One such site is http://www.guiweb.com/index.shtml but there are others.

It's easy. Your customer pays the fee, you email them the access code and they can log on and take your course as they choose. That's it!

Consulting. Consulting is the biggest fish in the pond! No matter what your topic is, you can teach it. Consulting is when you teach a group of people or an organization your subject, coaching can also be done in groups. You can easily incorporate either or both into your product line.

I am very much a person that will always remove the time for money equation from my business. I very seldom will work for a one-on-one situation unless there is a lot of money involved and I suggest once you are comfortable with selling your information products you take this route too.

It is much more profitable, less stressful and you can work when you want from where you want, when you eliminate time for money and one-on-one customers.

Pricing Your Products.

You must price your products in accordance to how much value
you are giving your customers. I know there are companies that
will sell a 6 set CD home study course for very minimal amount
of money, even as low as $99.00.

I totally advise against that type of pricing. If you want to
make a high 6 figure income and more you must be prepared
to ask for higher prices and I know people will happily pay you
these prices day in and day out.

I will say that, until you get your confidence and selling
skills up, you can charge lower prices but it should not be for
very long. You must sell your information by the value that you
can give your customer.

If my information product could, for example, bring my
customers in and extra $5,000.00 per month for just a few hours
a week is that not worth more than $99.00?

If I could show you how to make an extra $7,000.00 a
month for part-time work, what would that be worth to you? I
don't know about you but that would be worth a lot to me and
I think it would be worth a lot to many people. This would be
especially true if you could prove your point through happy
customers doing it and giving you testimonials.

I bet something like this would be worth $5,000.00 or more
so if you sold it for $2,700.00 that could be real value or even
a bargain to anyone. This is just an example but this is the way
you should sell your information so as to get you higher prices.

If I could take you by the hand and show you in a weekend
seminar how to make a 6 figure income from your book after
you have written it what would that be worth? Do you see how
you can create value for your information products?

Your Sales Funnel

Most sales funnels will start by having customers opt-in for a free report etc. After that, you may have them buy a $47.00 information product. Next, you would maybe have a $997.00 home study course and then a $2,000.00 or $3,000.00 take you by the hand weekend seminar.

EXAMPLE SALES FUNNEL

Your book

Opt In Offer
FREE MP3/FREE E-BOOK/FREE REPORT

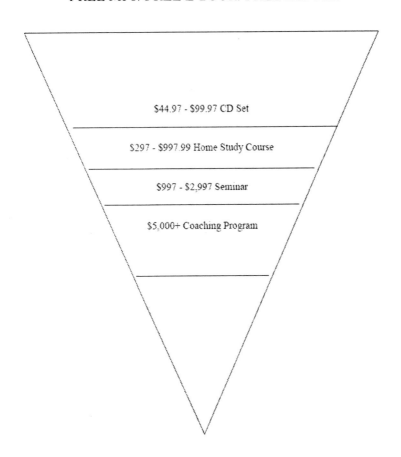

$44.97 - $99.97 CD Set

$297 - $997.99 Home Study Course

$997 - $2,997 Seminar

$5,000+ Coaching Program

The number of people that sign up for each more expensive product maybe a lot less but the profits will go through the roof for you. Think about it, if you charge $2,000.00 for a weekend seminar and 50 people come that is still $100,000.00 for a two day weekend. Don't forget you will be able to sell a video version of the same weekend that will even increase profits more.

One of the biggest stumbling blocks you may have is getting over just how many people will pay those prices. They do and they do all the time because you are giving value and changing lives. Try it you will be very pleased and much richer.

If you are unsure and unconfident on how to move yourself through this process go to our forum at: www. ExpertAuthorPublishing.com I know there will be someone who will be happy to help you through the process if you are still unsure how to do it at this point.

You want to introduce your customers to your least expensive products first and gradually work them up to the larger price points. Why? Because that's generally how people buy and you have to earn their trust.

Opt-in	Free MP3, Special Report etc.
CD	Free But must pay for shipping
6 CD set	$147.00 to $297.00
Home Study	$$297.00 to $997.00
Coaching programs	$5,000.00 and up

The way you put your sales funnel together is infinite. Be creative and most of all give more in value to your customers that you charge in dollars and you will do just fine.

Another very important strategy to add profits to your information empire is through affiliate marketing. Some marketers use this strategy only and make a high 6 figure income each year.

AFFILIATE MARKETING.

We talked earlier about having affiliates market for you. They send customers to your website and when the customer makes a purchase, the affiliate earns a commission. It's a great way to expand your customer base and increase your opt-in list.

However, you can also consider becoming an affiliate yourself.

WHAT IS AFFILIATE MARKETING?

Of course, before you add the title "Affiliate Marketer" to your resume, you need to understand what it is. An affiliate marketer is someone (you) that promotes and sells a company's products or services in exchange for a commission. The great thing about affiliate marketing is that there is no risk, no inventory, and the majority of the companies provide any sales material, links, or advertisements that you might need.

What companies do you affiliate with? What products or services do you support? For the information marketer, you need to be choosy with the products that you support. You need to find quality products that fit well into your niche. Remember that you don't want to lose your customer's respect or trust.

How To Find affiliate products.

Now that you have your chosen topic or niche, you need to find products to sell, right? Right! Your next step is to select a few good products to promote on your website or through your list.

Here's how to find them:

- Type your topic plus the word affiliate into your search engine. It will look like this +Dog Training + Affiliate. Make sure to use the plus sign because it tells the search engine that both words must be present on the website. Your search should generate several products that you can begin to research.

- You can also visit affiliate directories. These are websites that have affiliate products registered and categorized. This makes it easy for you to search for relevant products to sell on your website. To find an affiliate directory, simply type affiliate directory into your search engine. There are several good ones with thousands of products to choose from.

RESEARCHING AFFILIATE COMPANIES. WHAT TO LOOK FOR.

When adding affiliate companies to your portfolio remember you will want to protect your good reputation so only consider high quality products and services. You're recommending these products to people and you want them to come back and buy more from you.

You should also investigate the merchant's site and make sure that ordering and fulfilment are handled professionally.

Try to represent products where your affiliate link takes your customers directly to the company's order page and not their home page. Conversion rates sink rapidly if your customer has to hunt around on another web site to find the product.

Make sure that you understand the payment method. Do you get paid per sale or paid per lead? You'll also want to make sure that your commission is at least 10-20% of the cost of the product. Consider electronic downloadable products as well because your commissions can be a high as 75%

You shouldn't have to pay to be an affiliate and all affiliate support should be detailed in a guide. Look for companies that provide sales and marketing materials for you to use in your promotions.

Bonus items are companies that pay you if you send them another affiliate—this is called a two tier commission. Additionally, look for companies that offer lifetime cookies. If a customer visits their site but doesn't buy but comes back next month or in six months, do you get the commission?

How To Incorporate Affiliate Marketing Into Your Product Line

The best way to profit from affiliate products isn't necessarily to sell the products directly on your website with an advertisement but to actually write helpful and informative content and embed relevant links into the copy.

For example, if you're writing an article about how to stop your dog from jumping on people or how to stop your dog from barking, then you can promote certain products with a reference to them in the copy and a link. You can link to a training clicker or a reference and link to certain dog treat that you promote.

If you are affiliated with numerous products, don't try to cram all of the links into each article. Pick and choose, and respect your customers. First and foremost, you must make each article helpful and provide a benefit to your customer. Then and only then will they trust you and purchase from you or purchase an affiliated product.

Happiness is a choice

- Barry Neil Haufman

Conclusion

Your Path To Success

Once you start on your path to success as a published author you will find that there is lots of information available to you so as you can reach your goal quickly and simply. That being said, information overload and mindset can be your two biggest obstacles.

Being an author and selling information means that you, like me, are probably an information addict. Stay on focus with your niche and don't be distracted by all the information clutter.

Information marketers are very good at selling information because that is their business but don't get sidetracked by information that can take you off course for weeks. You will have time and money soon enough to try all the opportunities that are out there, but make your niche work first. Trust me, entrepreneurial drift can be a very big and seductive problem.

Stay laser focused and on track with your burning desire and you will find that you life dramatically changes for the better in a very short time, Be careful who you surround your self with as well. Most people don't understand this business model and can unknowingly discourage you and you don't want that.

The business model in this book is being used by many people to quietly make millions of dollars every year. We have not provided merely theories, but very practical ways to make a six figure income, and higher, from writing and publishing your own book. Get support from the right people and you will do just fine.

So now you're on your way to becoming a self published author and achieving all of the rewards that come with it! You're on your way to achieving all that you ever dreamed of. You'll be earning more money, meeting new people, making new friends, improving the lives of people all around you and people that you have never met!

Publishing a book and becoming an author will do more than make you the expert; it will make your life dramatically better.

You have the tools. You know how to plan your book, you know how to get it done in a very short time, you know how to promote yourself, your website, and your book. You know how to set up your publishing business, design your book for optimal sales, and you know how to position yourself at the top of the book selling charts.

More importantly, you now have the steps and tools that you need to build your business beyond your first book. All the information you need is available so the only real thing that can defeat you is your own mind. Stay strong, focused and get support and your goals will be quickly achieved. You have everything that you need to get started building an information marketing empire.

So get started! Take Action!

Best of luck on achieving your hopes and dreams!

Sincerely,

Bob Burnham

PS. Write to me! I want to hear your success stories because this is the biggest reason I do what I do.

Resources

Book Catalogs:

- R.R. Bowker Company http://www.bowker.com
- Direct Marketing Association http://www.www.the-dma.org
- Gale Group http://www.galegroup.com
- The Writer, Inc http://www.writermag.com
- Writer's Digest Books http://www.writersdigest.com

Magazines that review books:

- Bookselling this week http://www.bookweb.org
- Foreword Magazine http://www.forewordmagazine.com
- Kirkus Reviews http://www.kirkusreviews.com
- Publisher's weekly http://www.publishersweekly.com

Book Reviewers:

- Midwest Book Review http://www.midwestbookreview.com
- New York Review of Books http://www.nybooks.com
- Washington Post Book World http://www.washingtonpost.com

Bookstore Distributors, for self-publishers:

- AMS http://www.advmkt.com
- Austin & Company http://www.austinandcompanyinc. com
- Biblio Distribution http://www.bibliodistribution.com
- Client Distribution Services http://www.cdsbooks.com
- National Book Network http://www.nbnbooks.com
- Publisher's Marketing Association http://www. pmaonline.org
- Rights & Distribution, Inc http://www.fellpub.com
- SCB Distributors http://www.scbdistributors.com

POD Printers:

- LighteningSource/Ingram Book Group http://www. lighteningprint.com
- BookSurge, LLC http://www.booksurge.com

POD Publishers:

- Profits Publishing http://profitspublishing.com
- Authorhouse http://www.authorhouse.com
- Infinity Publishing http://www.infinitypublishing.com
- Trafford Publishing http://www.trafford.com
- iUniverse http://www.iUniverse.com
- Xlibris http://www.xlibris.com

Where To Find Freelancers:

- Elancehttp://www.elance.com
- Scriptlance http://www.scriptlance.com
- WriterLance http://www.writerlance.com
- iFreelance http://www.iFreelance.com

Online Book Chains/Resellers/POD and Distribution

- http://advantage.amazon.com/gp/vendor/public/ join-advantagbooks
- http://www.barnesandnoble.com/help/cds2.asp?PID= 8148&linkid=9&z=y&cds2Pid=9481
- ISBN http://www.isbn.org/standards/home/isbn/us/ secureapp.asp
- Library of Congress Number. http://www.copyright. gov.
- Copyright Registration. http://www.loc.gov/ copyright/forms

Direct Marketing/Copy Writing Resources

- Direct Marketing Association http://www.www.the-dma.org
- Gale Group http://www.galegroup.com
- The Writer, Inc http://www.writermag.com
- Writer's Digest Books http://www.writersdigest.com

Article websites:

- http://ezinearticles.com
- http://www.goarticles.com
- http://www.articledashboard.com/
- http://www.articlefinders.com/
- http://www.articlefinders.com/
- http://www.ideamarketers.com/
- http://www.articlealley.com/
- http://www.articledepot.co.uk/
- http://www.certificate.net/
- http://www.amazines.com/

Recommended Products and Coaches

- http://www.johnchilders.com/speakertraining.htm
- http://www.rmacart.com/
- http://www.bestsellermentoring.com
- http://marketingresultscoach.com
- http://www.writershelper.com/mentor.html

Website Promotion and Tools

- http://www.prweb.com/
- http://www.templatemonster.com/
- http://www.templatesbox.com/
- http://www.ezinedirectory.com
- http://inventory.overture.com/d/searchinventory/suggestion/
- http://www/1shoppingcart
- http://shopping-cart-review.toptenreviews.com
- http://www.aweber.com/?214107
- http://www.guiweb.com/index.shtml

If you are unsure and unconfident on how to move yourself through this self publishing process go to our forum at: www.ExpertAuthorPublishing.com

Good Books For Authors, Self Publishers, and Marketers to Own:

Chicago Manual of Style 15th edition Published by the University of Chicago Press

Writer's Market 2006 or 2007 Writer's Digest Books

Strunk & White The Elements of Style Copyright 2000 Allyn and Bacon, publishers

Thesaurus

Dictionary

Good General Information For Non-Fiction Writers:

100 Things Every Writer Needs To Know by Scott Edelstein
Copyright 1999 Penguin Putnam

How To Write a Book Proposal by Michael Larson Copyright
1997 Writer's Digest Books

100 ways to improve your writing by Gary Provost Copyright
1985 Mentor Publishing

The Craft of Research by Wayne C Booth, Gregory Colomb,
and Joseph Williams Copyright 2003 University of Chicago
Press

The Book on Writing by Paula LaRocque Copyright 2003
Marion Street Press

Good General Information For Fiction Writers:

Discovering the Writer Within by Bruce Ballenger and Barry
Lane Copyright 1999 Writer's Digest Books

Stephen King On Writing Copyright 2000 Pocket Books

Writing Fiction by Janet Burroway Copyright 2000 Addison
Wesley Longman

Anybody Can Write by Jean Bryant Copyright 1985 Whatever
Publishing

Immediate Fiction by Jerry Cleaver Copyright 2002 St. Martins

Creating Fiction Associated Writing Programs Copyright 1999
Storypress

More Books On Publishing and Promotion

The Wealthy Writer by Michael Meanwell Copyright 2004
Writer's Digest Books

Dan Poynter's Self-Publishing Manual Copyright 2006 Para
Publishing

The Well Fed Writer by Peter Bowerman Copyright 2000
Fanove Publishing

No More Rejections by Alice Orr Copyright 2004 Writer's
Digest Books

The Copywriter's Handbook By Robert Bly Copyright 2005
Owl Books

Grammar

Eats, Shoots & Leaves by Lynne Truss Copyright 2003 Gotham
Books

The Writer's Digest Grammar Desk Reference Writer's Digest
Books Copyright 2005.